SIX SISTERS' STUFF

Copycat cooking

SIX SISTERS' STUFF

Copycat cooking

100+ POPULAR

RESTAURANT MEALS YOU CAN

MAKE AT HOME

SHADOW
MOUNTAIN

To Mom,

for instilling in us a love for good food.

Visit us at ShadowMountain.com

Library of Congress Cataloging-in-Publication Data
Names: Six Sisters' Stuff, issuing body.
Title: Copycat cooking with Six Sisters' Stuff : 100+ popular restaurant meals you can make at home / Six Sisters' Stuff.
Description: Salt Lake City, Utah : Shadow Mountain, [2018] | Includes index.
Identifiers: LCCN 2017050724 | ISBN 9781629724430 (paperbound)
Subjects: LCSH: Cooking, American. | LCGFT: Cookbooks.
Classification: LCC TX715 .C793 2018 | DDC 641.5973—dc23
LC record available at https://lccn.loc.gov/2017050724

Printed in China
RR Donnelley, Shenzhen, China

10   9   8   7   6   5   4   3   2   1

Contents

COPYCAT APPETIZERS & SIDE DISHES

COPYCAT MAIN DISHES

COPYCAT DESSERTS

COPYCAT DRINKS

COPYCAT

Appetizers & Side Dishes

IN-N-OUT ANIMAL STYLE FRIES

Prep time: 10 minutes | Cook time: 23 minutes | Total time: 33 minutes | Makes: 6 to 8 servings

- 1 (32-ounce) bag frozen shoestring French fries
- 2 tablespoons vegetable oil
- 2 tablespoons brown sugar
- 1 yellow onion, diced
- 2 cups shredded cheddar cheese
- 1 recipe Fry Sauce

Bake fries according to package directions. While fries are baking, heat oil and brown sugar in a frying pan over medium heat. Add diced onion and stir frequently until caramelized, about 15 to 20 minutes. Remove fries from oven and sprinkle with cheese. Return to oven and broil on high for 3 minutes, or until cheese has melted and fries are golden brown around the edges.

To serve, top cheese fries with caramelized onions and Fry Sauce.

FRY SAUCE

- ½ cup mayonnaise
- ⅓ cup ketchup
- 1½ tablespoons pickle relish
- ½ teaspoon sugar
- ¼ teaspoon ground black pepper
- ¼ teaspoon salt
- ½ teaspoon apple cider vinegar

In a small bowl, whisk together mayonnaise, ketchup, pickle relish, sugar, pepper, salt, and apple cider vinegar until combined.

PANDA EXPRESS CREAM CHEESE RANGOONS

Prep time: 10 minutes | Cook time: 10 minutes | Total time: 20 minutes | Makes: 24 rangoons

Vegetable oil, for frying

1 **(8-ounce) package cream cheese, softened**

2 **tablespoons thinly sliced green onions**

¼ **teaspoon garlic powder**

24 **wonton wrappers**

1 **bottle sweet-and-sour sauce, for dipping**

Fill a medium pot with 2 to 3 inches of vegetable oil and heat to 350 degrees F.

In a mixing bowl, beat together cream cheese, green onions, and garlic powder. Spoon one teaspoon of cream cheese mixture onto each wonton wrapper. Dip finger in water and outline the outer edge of each wonton. Bring all corners of the wontons together and pinch in the center. Drop prepared wontons a few at a time into hot oil and fry until golden brown. Carefully remove wontons and drain briefly on paper towels before serving. Serve with sweet-and-sour sauce.

TEXAS ROADHOUSE ROLLS WITH CINNAMON HONEY BUTTER

Prep time: 2 hours | Cook time: 15 minutes | Total time: 2 hours 15 minutes | Makes: 24 rolls

1¼ cups milk	1 egg
2¼ teaspoons active dry yeast	1 teaspoon salt
1 teaspoon sugar	4 cups all-purpose flour
¼ cup honey	1 recipe Cinnamon Honey Butter
4 tablespoons butter, melted	

In a saucepan over medium-high heat, bring milk to a boil. Remove from heat and let cool to luke-warm.

In a mixing bowl, combine warm milk, yeast, sugar, and honey. Let sit for 5 minutes or until yeast is activated.

In a large bowl, combine yeast mixture, melted butter, egg, and salt. Mix in flour one cup at a time and stir until smooth.

Knead for 8 minutes by hand or in the bowl of an electric stand mixer.

Place dough onto a lightly floured surface and knead for 3 to 5 more minutes.

Spray a large bowl with nonstick cooking spray, place dough inside and cover with plastic wrap. Let rise for 1 hour in a warm place.

Punch down dough and roll out on a lightly floured surface until ½-inch thick. Cut into 24 squares and place on 2 large baking sheets sprayed with nonstick cooking spray. Cover with plastic wrap and let rise for 30 to 40 minutes or until doubled in size.

Preheat oven to 350 degrees F. and bake 12 to 15 minutes, or until lightly golden brown.

Brush melted butter on top of hot rolls, if desired.

CINNAMON HONEY BUTTER

| ½ | cup butter, softened | ½ | cup honey |
| ½ | cup powdered sugar | 1 | teaspoon ground cinnamon |

Beat together butter, powdered sugar, honey, and cinnamon until smooth; serve with warm rolls.

TEXAS ROADHOUSE CACTUS BLOSSOM

Prep time: 10 minutes | Cook time: 10 minutes | Total time: 20 minutes | Makes: 4 servings

Vegetable oil, for frying

1 egg, beaten

1 cup milk

1 cup all-purpose flour

1½ teaspoons salt

1½ teaspoons cayenne pepper

1 teaspoon paprika

½ teaspoon ground black pepper

¼ teaspoon dried oregano

⅛ teaspoon dried thyme

⅛ teaspoon ground cumin

1 large Vidalia onion

1 recipe Dipping Sauce

Fill a large pot with water and bring to a boil while prepping recipe. Fill a large bowl with cold water and set aside.

In a medium bowl, whisk together egg and milk; set aside. In a medium bowl, combine flour, salt, cayenne pepper, paprika, black pepper, dried oregano, dried thyme, and ground cumin; set aside.

Prepare your onion by cutting off both ends and peeling away the outermost layer of the onion. Use an apple corer or sharp knife to remove the center of the onion, approximately 1 inch in diameter. Using a large, sharp knife, begin cutting your petals. Cut directly across the center of the onion, cutting ¾ of the way down. Rotate your onion 90 degrees and cut directly across the onion again. Keep slicing each section in half until the onion has been cut 16 times, making sure to not cut more than ¾ of the way through the onion.

Place the onion in boiling water for 30 seconds. Remove onion and place in the cold water for 30 seconds; remove and dry off with a paper towel. Spread apart onion petals and place onion in milk mixture; remove and then coat completely in flour mixture, making sure to get mixture in between each petal. Dip in milk mixture again and coat in the flour mixture again.

Fill a large pot with 2 to 3 inches of vegetable oil and heat to 350 degrees F. Place onion right side up in hot oil for 10 minutes, or until the coating is golden brown and crispy and onion is soft on the inside. Serve with Dipping Sauce.

DIPPING SAUCE

½	cup mayonnaise	¼	teaspoon salt
¼	cup ketchup	⅛	teaspoon dried oregano
1	tablespoon horseradish sauce	⅛	teaspoon ground black pepper
¼	teaspoon paprika	¼	teaspoon cayenne pepper

In a medium bowl, whisk together mayonnaise, ketchup, horseradish sauce, paprika, salt, oregano, black pepper, and cayenne pepper until well combined.

THE CHEESECAKE FACTORY AVOCADO EGG ROLLS

Prep time: 10 minutes | Cook time: 5 to 8 minutes | Total time: 18 minutes | Makes: 8 servings

Vegetable oil, for frying

3 **avocados, diced**

¼ **cup minced red onion**

2 **tablespoons diced sun-dried tomatoes**

1 **tablespoon chopped cilantro**

¼ **teaspoon salt**

8 **egg-roll wrappers**

1 **recipe Avocado Egg Roll Dipping Sauce**

Fill a large pot with 2 to 3 inches of vegetable oil and heat to 375 degrees F. In a medium bowl, gently combine avocado, red onion, sun-dried tomatoes, cilantro, and salt. Distribute filling evenly onto the center of each egg-roll wrapper. Dip finger in water and outline the outer edge of each egg roll wrapper. Fold in opposite corners of the egg roll and pinch together in the center, then roll up from one side to the other. Fold top corner over the outside of the egg roll and press to seal. Repeat with remaining egg rolls. Deep-fry the egg rolls for 5 to 8 minutes or until golden brown. Drain on a plate covered with a paper towel. Serve warm with prepared Dipping Sauce.

AVOCADO EGG ROLL DIPPING SAUCE

½ **cup honey**

1 **teaspoon balsamic vinegar**

3 **teaspoons white vinegar**

½ **teaspoon lime juice**

½ **cup chopped cilantro**

2 **teaspoons minced garlic**

1 **green onion, minced**

1 **tablespoon sugar**

½ **teaspoon ground black pepper**

1 **teaspoon cumin**

¼ **cup olive oil**

In a medium bowl, whisk together honey, balsamic vinegar, white vinegar, and lime juice. Place bowl in the microwave and heat for 1 minute. Pulse cilantro, garlic, green onion, sugar, pepper, cumin, and olive oil in a food processor or blender until smooth. Add pureed mixture to honey mixture and whisk together.

OUTBACK STEAKHOUSE COCONUT SHRIMP

Prep time: 15 minutes | Cook time: 7 minutes | Total time: 22 minutes | Makes: 4 servings

1 (16-ounce) bag large frozen cooked shrimp

½ cup all-purpose flour

½ cup cornstarch

½ tablespoon salt

½ tablespoon white pepper

1 cup cold water

2 tablespoons vegetable oil
Vegetable oil, for frying

3 cups sweetened shredded coconut

1 recipe Marmalade Dipping Sauce

Preheat oven to 400 degrees F.

Rinse off the shrimp and pat dry; set aside. In a medium mixing bowl, combine flour, cornstarch, salt, and white pepper. Add water and 2 tablespoons vegetable oil; whisk together until well blended; set aside.

Heat 2 to 3 inches oil in a large pot until oil reaches 325 degrees F.

Place coconut on a small cookie sheet or pan. Dip each shrimp in the batter and then roll in the shredded coconut. Fry shrimp in hot oil just until they start to turn golden brown. Place fried shrimp on a large cookie sheet and bake in hot oven 5 minutes to finish cooking. Serve with Marmalade Dipping Sauce.

MARMALADE DIPPING SAUCE

1 cup orange marmalade

⅛ cup Dijon mustard

⅓ cup honey

1 teaspoon hot sauce

Combine the orange marmalade, Dijon mustard, honey, and hot sauce. Mix together well.

PANDA EXPRESS CHOW MEIN

Prep time: 15 minutes | Cook time: 10 minutes | Total time: 25 minutes | Makes: 4 to 6 servings

1 (8-ounce) package long, uncooked chow mein noodles

2 tablespoons sesame oil, divided

4 ribs celery, finely sliced

½ yellow onion, finely sliced

1 cup shredded cabbage

¼ cup shredded carrot

2 tablespoons rice vinegar

3 tablespoons soy sauce, plus more to taste

Cook chow mein noodles according to package directions; set aside. In a large skillet or wok, heat 1 tablespoon sesame oil over high heat. Add celery, onion, cabbage, and carrot and stir fry until soft and edges of cabbage start to brown. Add rice vinegar (it will sizzle) and stir for a few seconds. Add cooked chow mein noodles to the pan and toss with 1 tablespoon sesame oil and soy sauce. Add more or less soy sauce, depending how strong you want the flavor. Stir until everything is warm, and serve.

APPLEBEE'S MOZZARELLA STICKS

Prep time: 50 minutes | Cook time: 10 minutes | Total time: 1 hour | Makes: 24 sticks

12 sticks part-skim mozzarella string cheese

¼ cup Italian breadcrumbs

¼ cup panko breadcrumbs

1 teaspoon dried parsley

¼ teaspoon dried basil

⅛ teaspoon dried oregano

⅛ teaspoon garlic powder

¼ cup all-purpose flour

1 large egg

Marinara sauce or ranch dressing, for dipping

Cut string cheese sticks in half and freeze until hard, about 30 minutes. Meanwhile, in a small bowl, combine the breadcrumbs, panko breadcrumbs, parsley, basil, oregano, and garlic powder; set aside. In a separate bowl, add the flour; set aside. In a third bowl, add the egg and whisk well. Spray a large baking sheet with nonstick cooking spray. Dip frozen cheese sticks in the flour, shaking off any excess flour.

Next, dip sticks in the egg and then coat with the breadcrumbs mixture, coating completely. Place sticks on prepared baking sheet. When all of the sticks are coated, freeze on the sheet for at least 15 minutes, or until ready to bake. When ready to bake, preheat oven to 400 degrees F.

Bake 4 to 5 minutes, turn sticks over, and bake an additional 4 to 5 minutes, or until sticks are golden brown and soft. Serve warm with marinara sauce or ranch dressing.

CHILI'S SKILLET QUESO

Prep time: 5 minutes | Cook time: 5 minutes | Total time: 10 minutes | Makes: 8 to 10 servings

1 (16-ounce) box Velveeta cheese

1 cup milk

2 teaspoons paprika

½ teaspoon ground cayenne pepper

1 (15-ounce) can chili without beans

4 teaspoons chili powder

1 tablespoon lime juice

½ teaspoon ground cumin

Cut the Velveeta cheese into cubes. Combine the cheese with the remaining ingredients in a medium saucepan over medium heat. Stir frequently until cheese melts. Enjoy with tortilla chips or bread.

OLIVE GARDEN SPINACH ARTICHOKE DIP

Prep time: 10 minutes | Cook time: 25 minutes | Total time: 35 minutes | Makes: 8 servings

- 1 **(8-ounce) package light cream cheese, room temperature**
- ¼ **cup mayonnaise**
- ½ **cup shredded Parmesan cheese**
- 1 **garlic clove, crushed**
- ½ **teaspoon dried basil**

- ½ **teaspoon garlic salt**
- **Salt and pepper to taste**
- 1 **(14-ounce) can artichoke hearts, drained and chopped**
- ½ **cup frozen chopped spinach**
- ¼ **cup shredded mozzarella cheese**

Preheat oven to 350 degrees F. Spray a 9-inch pie pan with nonstick cooking spray and set aside.

In a large bowl, mix together cream cheese, mayonnaise, Parmesan cheese, garlic, basil, garlic salt, and salt and pepper. Fold in the artichoke hearts and spinach and mix until completely blended.

Pour dip into prepared pie pan and top with mozzarella cheese. Bake 25 minutes, or until the top turns golden brown.

Serve with thinly sliced Italian bread.

RAINFOREST CAFE BEEF LAVA NACHOS

Prep time: 20 minutes | Cook time: 15 minutes | Total time: 35 minutes | Makes: 8 to 10 servings

1½ pounds lean ground beef

1 yellow onion, diced

1 (1-ounce) packet taco seasoning

⅓ cup water

1 (10-ounce) bag tortilla chips

1 (14-ounce) can black beans, rinsed and drained

1 red bell pepper, diced

1 green bell pepper, diced

1½ cups shredded Monterey Jack cheese

1½ cups shredded cheddar cheese

3 teaspoons sliced green onions

½ cup sour cream

1 cup pico de gallo (or favorite salsa)

½ cup guacamole

In a large skillet over medium-high heat, brown ground beef and onion until beef is no longer pink. Add in taco seasoning and water, reduce heat to low, and let simmer 4 to 5 minutes.

On a large platter, spread out a single layer of tortilla chips. Top with half of the beef mixture, half of the black beans, half of the green and red bell peppers, half of each cheese, and half of the green onions. Repeat layers.

Place nachos in microwave and heat for 60 seconds or until the cheese starts to melt; or, place in an oven at 350 degrees F. until the cheese starts to melt.

Top nachos off with sour cream, pico de gallo, and guacamole.

Serve immediately.

BUFFALO WILD WINGS GARLIC PARMESAN WINGS

Prep time: 15 minutes | Cook time: 30 minutes | Total time: 45 minutes | Makes: 4 to 6 servings

- 1 pound bone-in chicken wings
- 6 cloves garlic, peeled
- 1 tablespoon olive oil
- ½ cup mayonnaise
- 2 tablespoons grated Parmesan cheese
- 1 tablespoon light corn syrup
- 1 teaspoon lemon juice
- 2 teaspoons vinegar
- ¼ teaspoon ground oregano
- ¼ teaspoon dried basil
- ¼ teaspoon ground black pepper
- ½ teaspoon salt
- ½ teaspoon crushed red pepper flakes

Preheat oven to 400 degrees F. Line chicken wings on a large baking sheet and bake 35 to 45 minutes, or until internal temperature reaches 165 degrees F. and the outside is crispy.

Place the garlic cloves in a small baking dish and drizzle with olive oil. Cover dish with aluminum foil and bake in oven with wings for 20 minutes or until garlic is tender.

Mix remaining ingredients in a medium bowl and stir until smooth. Crush cooled garlic and mix with prepared sauce.

Toss sauce with cooked wings and serve.

FAMOUS DAVE'S CORNBREAD MUFFINS

Prep time: 10 minutes | Cook time: 20 minutes | Total time: 30 minutes | Makes: 16 muffins

1¾ cups cornmeal

1½ cups all-purpose flour

2 teaspoons baking powder

¾ teaspoon salt

¼ teaspoon baking soda

2 eggs

¾ cup sugar

¼ cup butter-flavored shortening

½ teaspoon vanilla extract

1 cup milk

⅓ cup vegetable oil

¼ cup honey

Butter, for topping

Preheat oven to 400 degrees F. Line a muffin pan with 16 liners and set aside.

In a large bowl, mix together cornmeal, flour, baking powder, salt, and baking soda.

In a separate medium bowl, cream together eggs, sugar, shortening, and vanilla with an electric mixer. Pour the wet ingredients into the bowl with the dry ingredients and stir. Add in milk, vegetable oil, and honey. Mix well until batter is smooth.

Fill each muffin cup about ¾ full and bake 18 to 20 minutes (watch for the tops to turn golden).

Remove from oven and top each muffin with butter while they are hot so that the butter can melt and sink into the muffin.

TGI FRIDAYS GREEN BEAN FRIES

Prep time: 15 | Cook time: 5 | Total time: 20 minutes | Makes: 6 servings

Vegetable oil, for frying

1 pound fresh green beans, trimmed

2 cups chicken broth

2 eggs

1 cup milk

1 cup all-purpose flour

1 cup breadcrumbs

½ teaspoon onion powder

1 teaspoon garlic powder

Salt and pepper to taste

Heat a few cups vegetable oil in a deep pot or fryer over medium-high heat.

Pour chicken broth into a saucepan and bring to a boil over medium-high heat.

Add the green beans and let boil for 5 minutes.

Remove beans from broth with a slotted spoon and set in a bowl of cold water.

After beans are cooled down, pat dry with a paper towel.

Whisk the eggs and milk together in a shallow bowl.

In another shallow bowl, combine flour, breadcrumbs, onion powder, garlic powder, salt, and pepper.

Dip the beans into the egg mixture, followed by the flour mixture, and place in hot oil, a few beans at a time. Cook 2 to 3 minutes or until golden brown.

Serve with ranch dressing or other dipping sauces.

TGI FRIDAYS LOADED POTATO SKINS

Prep time: 10 minutes | Cook time: 16 minutes | Total time: 26 minutes | Makes: 8

- 4 **large russet potatoes, baked**
- 3 **tablespoons olive oil**
- 1 **tablespoon grated Parmesan cheese**
- ½ **teaspoon salt**
- ¼ **teaspoon garlic powder**
- ¼ **teaspoon paprika**
- ⅛ **teaspoon ground black pepper**
- 8 **bacon strips, cooked and crumbled**
- 1½ **cups shredded cheddar cheese**
- ½ **cup sour cream**
- 4 **green onions, sliced**

Preheat oven to 475 degrees F.

Cut potatoes in half lengthwise; scoop out pulp, leaving a ¼-inch shell. Discard pulp or reserve for another recipe. Place potatoes skins on a greased baking sheet. Combine oil, Parmesan cheese, salt, garlic powder, paprika, and pepper; brush over both sides of skins.

Bake 7 minutes; turn over. Bake until crisp, about 7 minutes more.

Sprinkle bacon and cheddar cheese inside skins. Bake 2 minutes longer or until the cheese is melted.

Top with sour cream and onions. Serve immediately.

MACARONI GRILL ROSEMARY BREAD

Prep time: 3 hours | Cook time: 20 minutes | Total time: 3 hours 20 minutes | Makes: 6 servings

- 2 **teaspoons active dry yeast**
- 2 **teaspoons sugar**
- 1 **cup warm water, divided**
- 1 **tablespoon extra-virgin olive oil, plus extra for bowl and brushing bread**

- 2 **tablespoons dried rosemary, divided**
- 2½ **cups all-purpose flour, plus more for dusting**
- 1½ **teaspoons kosher salt**
- **Freshly ground pepper to taste**

Combine the yeast, sugar, and ¼ cup warm water in a large bowl. Let stand for 5 minutes, until foamy.

In the same bowl, add 1 tablespoon olive oil, 1½ tablespoons rosemary, salt, ¾ cups warm water, and all the flour.

Mix until dough forms.

Work dough by hand on a lightly floured surface for about 5 to 7 minutes.

Coat a bowl with olive oil and put the dough in. Cover with plastic wrap or towel and let stand 1 to 2 hours, or until doubled in size.

Once dough has doubled, place on a lightly floured surface. Divide dough in half. Work each half for another 1 to 2 minutes and place on a parchment-paper-lined baking sheet.

Let stand, uncovered, 1 to 2 hours or until dough has doubled again.

Once the dough has doubled, preheat oven to 400 degrees F. and bake 10 minutes.

Remove bread from oven and coat with a light layer of olive oil. Sprinkle kosher salt and rosemary on top.

Return to the oven and bake an additional 10 to 12 minutes.

Let cool slightly. Serve warm with a side of olive oil mixed with crushed black pepper.

LITTLE CAESARS CRAZY BREAD

Prep time: 10 minutes | Cook time: 8 minutes | Total time: 18 minutes | Makes: 16 breadsticks

1 (10-ounce) can refrigerated pizza dough

2 tablespoons butter, melted

½ teaspoon garlic salt

⅛ cup finely grated Parmesan cheese

Preheat oven to 450 degrees F.

Unroll dough on a clean surface. Cut dough in half lengthwise, then cut 8 strips vertically. Place each strip onto a lightly greased baking sheet.

Bake 6 to 8 minutes or until golden brown.

While bread sticks are baking, melt the butter and stir in garlic salt. Remove bread sticks from the oven and brush on garlic-butter mixture. Sprinkle with Parmesan cheese. Serve with marinara sauce for dipping.

OLIVE GARDEN BREADSTICKS

Prep time: 1 hour 5 minutes | Cook time: 12 to 15 minutes | Total time: 1 hour 17 minutes | Makes: 16 breadsticks

- 2 tablespoons sugar
- 1 packet active dry yeast
- 1½ cups warm water
- 3½ cups all-purpose flour, add more or less as needed

- 1 tablespoon salt
- 2 tablespoons unsalted butter, melted
- 1 recipe Butter Topping

In a large bowl, dissolve sugar and yeast in warm water and let sit 10 minutes, until frothy.

Add flour, salt, and melted butter to the yeast mixture. Mix with a wooden spoon until fully combined. Knead dough for a few minutes, just until dough is smooth in consistency.

Spray a cookie sheet with nonstick cooking spray. Pull off pieces of dough and roll out into strips. Cover the dough with a light towel and let sit in a warm place for 45 minutes to rise.

Preheat oven to 400 degrees F.

Bake breadsticks 6 to 7 minutes. Brush the breadsticks with half the Butter Topping. Return breadsticks to oven and bake 5 to 8 more minutes.

Remove breadsticks from oven, brush the other half of the Butter Topping on the sticks, and serve immediately.

BUTTER TOPPING

- ½ cup butter
- 2 teaspoons garlic powder
- 1 teaspoon salt

Melt butter, garlic powder, and teaspoon salt together in a small bowl.

KFC POTATO WEDGES

Prep time: 10 minutes | Cook time: 4 minutes | Total time: 14 minutes | Makes: 5 servings

1 cup milk	¼ teaspoon paprika
1 egg	½ teaspoon garlic powder
1 cup all-purpose flour	½ teaspoon garlic salt
2 tablespoons seasoned salt	5 large russet potatoes
1 teaspoon ground black pepper	Canola oil, for frying

In a bowl, whisk the egg and milk together until smooth and fully combined. In a separate bowl, combine flour, seasoned salt, black pepper, paprika, garlic powder, and garlic salt. Cut potatoes into ½-inch thick wedges and place them in the egg-and-milk mixture. In a large pot, heat the canola oil until it reaches 375 degrees F. Take about 5 to 6 potato wedges at a time out of the egg-and-milk mixture and place in the flour mixture; toss until coated. Place coated wedges in the hot oil and fry 3 to 4 minutes, flipping occasionally until they reach the desired golden texture. Repeat with remaining wedges.

KFC COLESLAW

Prep time: 10 minutes | Makes: 6 to 8 servings

½ cup Miracle Whip

⅓ cup sugar

¼ cup milk

¼ cup buttermilk

2½ tablespoons lemon juice

1½ tablespoons white vinegar

½ teaspoon salt

⅛ teaspoon ground black pepper

1 head cabbage, finely chopped

¼ cup finely chopped carrot

2 tablespoons minced onion

In a medium bowl, whisk together Miracle Whip, sugar, milk, buttermilk, lemon juice, vinegar, salt, and pepper; set aside. In a large bowl, combine cabbage, carrots, and onion and toss together. Pour dressing over the slaw and mix until well combined. Cover and refrigerate at least 4 hours before serving for best results.

P.F. CHANG'S CHICKEN LETTUCE WRAPS

Prep time: 15 minutes | Cook time: 25 minutes | Total time: 40 minutes | Makes: 4 servings

1 **pound ground chicken**	¼ **cup chopped green onion**
1 **tablespoon olive oil**	½ **cup chopped water chestnuts**
⅓ **cup soy sauce**	**Dash freshly grated ginger**
⅓ **cup teriyaki sauce**	1 **teaspoon minced garlic**
¼ **cup rice wine vinegar**	**Salt and pepper**
1 **cup chopped mushrooms**	1 **teaspoon garlic salt**
½ **yellow onion, chopped**	4 **romaine lettuce leaves**

Brown ground chicken in a medium skillet over medium heat until cooked through. Add olive oil, soy sauce, teriyaki sauce, rice wine vinegar, mushrooms, onion, green onion, water chestnuts, ginger, garlic, salt and pepper, and garlic salt and sauté, stirring often, until the onions are soft and translucent. Remove from heat and serve in lettuce leaves. Serve as main dish or appetizer.

CHICK-FIL-A SUPERFOOD SIDE SALAD

Prep time: 15 minutes | Makes: 8 servings

6 cups chopped kale

2 cups chopped broccoli

⅓ cup sunflower seeds

½ cup dried cherries

½ cup apple cider vinegar

⅓ cup olive oil

1 tablespoon honey

4 tablespoons pure maple syrup

1 teaspoon sugar

¼ teaspoon freshly ground black pepper

¼ teaspoon salt

In a medium-large bowl, combine kale, broccoli florets, sunflower seeds, and dried cherries. In a small bowl, whisk together cider vinegar, olive oil, honey, maple syrup, sugar, pepper, and salt until fully combined. Pour dressing over the salad and toss until the leaves and broccoli are shiny and coated. Refrigerate for 3 hours, or let sit overnight, so the flavor is set into the salad. Serve cold and enjoy!

CHIPOTLE CORN SALSA

Prep time: 10 minutes | Makes: 6 servings

1 **(16-ounce) bag white sweet corn, thawed**

1 **large poblano pepper, diced**

1 **jalapeño pepper, seeded and diced**

1 **red onion, diced**

½ **cup chopped, fresh cilantro**

Juice of 2 limes

Large pinch sea salt

Dash pepper

In a medium bowl, combine the corn, diced peppers, onion, and cilantro. Toss until well combined. Drizzle with the lime juice and salt and pepper. Taste and add more salt and pepper according to preference. Serve with meat, chicken, nachos, or tortilla chips.

COPYCAT

Main Dishes

P.F. CHANG'S MONGOLIAN BEEF

Prep time: 10 minutes | Cook time: 10 minutes | Total time: 20 minutes | Makes: 6 servings

- 2 teaspoons vegetable oil, plus additional for frying
- ½ teaspoon minced ginger
- 1 tablespoon chopped garlic
- ½ cup soy sauce

- ½ cup water
- ¾ cup dark brown sugar
- 1 pound flank steak
- ¼ cup cornstarch
- 2 large green onions, chopped

Heat 2 teaspoons vegetable oil in a medium saucepan over medium-low heat. Add ginger and garlic to the pan and stir briefly, about 15 seconds. Stir in the soy sauce and water. Dissolve the brown sugar in the sauce, then increase the heat to medium and boil 2 to 3 minutes, or until the sauce thickens. Remove from heat and set aside.

Slice the flank steak against the grain into ¼-inch-thick, bite-size slices. Dip the steak pieces in the cornstarch to apply a very thin dusting to both sides of each piece of beef. Let the beef sit for about 10 minutes. As the beef sits, heat ½- to 1 inch oil in a large wok over medium heat until it's nice and hot, but not smoking. Add the beef and sauté until brown. Stir the meat so it cooks evenly. Cook about 3 minutes and then use a large slotted spoon to remove the meat and drain on paper towels. Dab any excess oil off meat with a paper towel. Add meat to saucepan with the sauce in it. Return pan to stovetop over medium heat. Add chopped green onions and let sauce simmer until warm. Serve over rice.

HONEYBAKED HAM

Prep time: 10 minutes | Cook time: 8 hours | Total time: 8 hours 10 minutes | Makes: 14 servings

1	(7- to 10-pound) spiral sliced ham	½	teaspoon ground cinnamon
½	cup brown sugar	2	tablespoons brown Dijon mustard
½	cup honey	⅓	cup water
¼	teaspoon ground nutmeg	2	tablespoons cornstarch

Spray slow cooker with nonstick cooking spray or line with a slow-cooker liner. Place ham in the slow cooker. In a medium saucepan over medium heat, whisk together sugar, honey, nutmeg, cinnamon, and mustard. Cook 2 to 5 minutes, until sugar is dissolved and mixture is combined well. Remove from heat. Pour water in the bottom of the slow cooker. Pour honey–brown sugar mixture over the ham.

Cover and cook the ham on low 6 to 8 hours. (If the ham is too large to use the slow cooker's lid, tent tightly with foil.) Baste the ham with the juices in the bottom of the slow cooker once every hour. Remove ham from slow cooker to a large platter and set aside. Pour the juices from the bottom of the slow cooker into a medium saucepan. Mix 2 tablespoons cornstarch with 1 tablespoon water and pour into the saucepan. Cook on medium heat until sauce starts to thicken. Use that as a glaze over the ham.

Note: To bake ham in the oven, place ham in a large roasting pan and cover with aluminum foil. Bake ham 15 to 20 minutes per pound at 350 degrees F. Baste the ham once every 30 minutes.

RUBY TUESDAY'S ASIAN GLAZED SALMON

Prep time: 10 minutes | Cook time: 9 minutes | Total time: 19 minutes | Makes: 4 servings

- 4 (4- to 6-ounce) salmon filets
- ½ cup brown sugar
- ½ cup soy sauce
- 2 tablespoons hoisin sauce

- 2 tablespoons ground ginger
- 2 teaspoons red pepper flakes
- 1 teaspoon ground black pepper
- 1 tablespoon lime juice

Preheat oven to 350 degrees F. Spray a glass baking dish with nonstick cooking spray.

Place salmon filets in prepared pan and set aside. Combine remaining ingredients in a small saucepan and heat until it begins to bubble. Pour hot glaze over salmon filets. Bake 8 to 10 minutes, or until fish flakes easily and is cooked through.

MIMI'S CAFE FRENCH POT ROAST

Prep time: 10 minutes | Cook time: 6 hours | Total time: 6 hours 10 minutes | Makes: 5 servings

- 1 (2- to 3-pound) chuck roast
- 2 tablespoons olive oil
- 2 tablespoons minced garlic
- 2 cups low-sodium beef broth
- 1 tablespoon Worcestershire sauce
- 1 teaspoon onion powder
- 2 tablespoons brown sugar
- 2 large onions, sliced
- 2 cups carrots
- 7 red potatoes, sliced
- 2 to 3 tablespoons cornstarch
- ⅓ cup water

Place chuck roast in a slow cooker. Combine olive oil, minced garlic, beef broth, Worcestershire sauce, onion powder, and brown sugar in a medium bowl until well combined. Pour the mixture over the roast in the slow cooker. Add the onion, carrots, and potatoes. Cover with lid and cook 6 hours on low. Remove meat and vegetables from the slow cooker and place one cup of the remaining juices in a pan. Add the cornstarch and water and whisk. Bring to a slight boil, then remove from heat and serve over roast and vegetables.

IKEA SWEDISH MEATBALLS

Prep time: 7 minutes | Cook time: 8 hours | Total time: 8 hours 7 minutes | Makes: 6 servings

- 1 (10.75-ounce) can cream of mushroom soup
- 2 cups beef broth
- 1 cup fresh, sliced mushrooms
- ½ cup diced onion
- 1 teaspoon garlic powder
- 2 tablespoons A.1. Steak Sauce
- 1 tablespoon Worcestershire sauce

- 2 tablespoons brown sugar
- ½ teaspoon paprika
- ½ teaspoon salt
- ½ teaspoon ground black pepper
- 1 (28-ounce) bag frozen homestyle meatballs
- 1 cup sour cream

Whisk together cream of mushroom soup and beef broth and pour in slow cooker. Add mushrooms, onion, garlic powder, steak sauce, Worcestershire sauce, brown sugar, paprika, salt, and pepper and mix until combined. Add meatballs and mix until meatballs are coated in sauce. Cover and cook on high 4 to 6 hours or low 8 to 10 hours. Mix in sour cream during the last 30 minutes of cooking. Serve over rice or mashed potatoes.

KNEADERS CHICKEN SALAD SANDWICHES

Prep time: 10 minutes | Cook time: 10 minutes | Total time: 20 minutes | Makes: 8 servings

¼ cup white vinegar

Salt to taste

Pepper to taste

1¼ cups mayonnaise

1¼ cups sour cream

4 ribs celery, chopped

1 bunch green onions, chopped

4 to 6 boneless, skinless chicken breasts, cooked and shredded

In a small bowl, combine vinegar, salt, pepper, mayonnaise, and sour cream. In a larger, separate bowl, mix celery, green onion, and chicken. Fold wet ingredients into chicken mixture. Chill in refrigerator overnight or for a few hours for the best flavor. Serve on buns, rolls, or croissants.

OLIVE GARDEN TUSCAN CHICKEN

Prep time: 20 minutes | Cook time: 25 minutes | Total time: 45 minutes | Makes: 4 servings

1 cup all-purpose flour

1½ tablespoons garlic salt

1 teaspoon ground black pepper

1 teaspoon dried basil

½ teaspoon Italian seasoning

½ teaspoon dried oregano

4 boneless skinless chicken breasts

7 tablespoons extra-virgin olive oil, divided

1 red bell pepper, cut into thin strips or chopped

1 tablespoon finely minced garlic

2½ tablespoons cornstarch, divided

½ cup low-sodium chicken broth

½ cup heavy cream

6 ounces fresh spinach

1 cup milk

1 cup freshly grated Parmesan cheese

1 (16-ounce) package fettuccine noodles

Preheat oven to 350 degrees F.

Combine flour, garlic salt, pepper, basil, Italian seasoning, and oregano in a shallow bowl. Dip each chicken breast in the flour mixture and coat well. In a large skillet, heat 5 tablespoons oil until hot. Place the breaded chicken in the oil until each side is golden. Don't cook all the way through; it will finish cooking in the oven.

Line a baking sheet with aluminum foil and spray with cooking spray. Place the chicken breasts on the cookie sheet and bake 15 minutes, until cooked through. Set aside until ready to use.

While the chicken is baking, prepare the noodles as directed on package. Wipe the skillet with some paper towels and add the remaining 2 tablespoons olive oil. Cook the diced red pepper and garlic for about 3 minutes. Stir in 1 tablespoon cornstarch and stir constantly for one minute. Add the chicken broth and bring to a light simmer while whisking constantly until it is starting to thicken, about 3 to 4 minutes. In a separate small bowl, whisk together the heavy cream and the rest of the cornstarch. Add the spinach, cream, and milk to the skillet. Bring this to a simmer and continue to cook until spinach starts to soften and go a dark-green color. Stir in the cheese.

Top the noodles with the breaded chicken and spoon the sauce on top.

PIZZA HUT DEEP DISH PIZZA

Prep time: 1 hour 25 minutes | Cook time: 15 minutes | Total time: 1 hour 40 minutes | Makes: 3 nine-inch pizzas

2½ teaspoons active dry yeast
1 tablespoon sugar
½ teaspoon salt
¼ cup nonfat dry milk
1⅓ cups warm water
2 tablespoons vegetable oil
4 cups all-purpose flour
1 (8-ounce) can tomato sauce

1 teaspoon dried oregano
½ teaspoon dried marjoram
½ teaspoon dried basil
½ teaspoon garlic salt
Salt and pepper to taste
3 cups shredded mozzarella cheese
Preferred toppings
6 tablespoons vegetable oil

In a large bowl, combine yeast, sugar, salt, and dry milk. Add warm water and stir until combined. Let sit for 3 to 5 minutes. Add 2 tablespoons vegetable oil and stir again. Add flour, one cup at a time, until dough forms. Knead dough on a lightly floured surface for 8 to 10 minutes, or use a stand mixer with a dough hook. Divide dough into three balls.

Pour 2 tablespoons vegetable oil into each of three 9-inch cake pans; use a brush to spread oil evenly along the bottom and sides of each pan. Roll out each dough ball into a 9-inch circle and place in prepared cake pans. Cover each pan with plastic wrap, place in a warm area, and allow to rise for 1 hour.

In a small bowl, whisk tomato sauce and seasonings until well combined.

Preheat oven to 475 degrees F. Spread ⅓ cup sauce on each pizza and top with 1 cup of shredded mozzarella cheese. Top with desired toppings and cook 10 to 15 minutes, or until crust is golden brown.

RED ROBIN BLEU RIBBON BURGER

Prep time: 10 minutes | Cook time: 10 minutes | Total time: 20 minutes | Makes: 4 servings

1 **pound ground beef**	4 **onion-flavored hamburger buns**
Hamburger seasoning to taste	**French-fried onions**
Steak sauce to taste	**Bleu cheese crumbles**
1 **teaspoon chipotle sauce**	1 **tomato, sliced**
½ **cup mayonnaise**	**Shredded lettuce**

Divide ground beef into 4 equal patties and season with hamburger seasoning. Grill patties to desired doneness. Remove from grill and brush with steak sauce, as desired. Whisk together chipotle sauce and mayonnaise and spread on the bottom half of each bun. Top with a handful of French fried onions. Place patties on top of onions and sprinkle on bleu cheese crumbles, as desired. Top with sliced tomato, shredded lettuce, and other half of bun.

THE CHEESECAKE FACTORY SUN-DRIED TOMATO FETTUCCINE

Prep time: 10 minutes | Cook time: 10 minutes | Total time: 20 minutes | Makes: 8 servings

1 (16-ounce) package fettuccine

2 tablespoons olive oil

4 teaspoons minced garlic

½ cup diced sun-dried tomatoes

1 (14.5-ounce) can petite diced tomatoes, drained

3 tablespoons tomato paste

1 tablespoon sugar

1 cup heavy cream

½ cup sour cream

2 cups baby spinach

Salt and pepper to taste

Cook fettuccine according to package directions, reserving 1 cup of the pasta water; set aside. While pasta is cooking, add olive oil to a large pot over medium-high heat. Sauté garlic for 1 minute, being careful not to burn the garlic. Add sun-dried tomatoes, diced tomatoes, tomato paste, and sugar, stirring until well combined. Reduce heat to medium-low and whisk in cream and sour cream. Let simmer and thicken for 5 minutes. Add spinach to sauce and cook until wilted. Add salt and pepper to taste. If sauce is too thick, use reserved pasta water to thin it out. Add pasta to prepared sauce and toss until coated.

BJ'S BREWHOUSE SWEET PIG PIZZA

Prep time: 30 minutes | Cook time: 20 minutes | Total time: 50 minutes | Makes: 2 fourteen-inch pizzas

- 2 cups warm water
- 1 tablespoon active dry yeast
- 5 cups all-purpose flour, divided
- 1 tablespoon salt
- 4 tablespoons olive oil, divided
- 1 cup marinara sauce, divided

- 4 cups shredded mozzarella, divided
- 1 cup diced cooked ham
- 1 cup diced, fresh pineapple
- 2 Roma tomatoes, diced
  Italian seasoning

In a large mixing bowl or the bowl of an electric stand mixer bowl, combine warm water and yeast; let sit 5 minutes, until yeast proofs. Add 2 cups flour and mix well. Add remaining 3 cups flour and salt and knead or mix until smooth. Cover bowl with plastic wrap and let rise for 20 minutes.

Pour 2 tablespoons olive oil into each of two 14-inch pizza pans and spread evenly. Remove dough, split in half, and roll out into two pizza crusts on a lightly floured surface. Place crusts onto pizza pans.

Preheat oven to 400 degrees F.

Spread ½ cup marinara sauce on top of each crust. Top each pizza with 2 cups shredded mozzarella, ½ cup diced ham, ½ cup diced pineapple, and 1 diced Roma tomato. Sprinkle Italian seasoning on top to taste and bake 18 to 20 minutes, or until crust is golden brown.

CHICK-FIL-A CHICKEN NUGGETS AND CHICK-FIL-A SAUCE

Prep time: 45 minutes | Cook time: 30 minutes | Total time: 1 hour 15 minutes | Makes: 4 servings

- 1 large egg
- 1 cup milk
- 1 pound boneless, skinless chicken breasts
- 1¼ cups all-purpose flour
- 2 tablespoons powdered sugar

- 2 teaspoons salt
- 1 teaspoon ground black pepper
- ½ teaspoon chili powder
  Canola oil, for frying
- 1 recipe Chick-fil-A Sauce

In a large bowl, whisk egg and milk together. Cut chicken into cubed, bite-size pieces, trimming off any fat. Put the chicken in the milk mixture and toss until well coated. Refrigerate at least 30 minutes.

In another large bowl, combine flour, powdered sugar, salt, pepper, and chili powder and stir; set aside. Pour 1 inch oil in a cast iron pot or large saucepan and heat over medium-high heat. Remove the chicken from refrigerator and place about 8 pieces in the flour mixture. Make sure chicken pieces are coated with the flour, then place them carefully into the hot oil. Cook each side for at least 2 to 3 minutes, or until golden brown and chicken is cooked through. Place chicken on paper towels to soak up any oil. Repeat the same steps with the rest of the chicken and serve with Chick-fil-A Sauce.

CHICK-FIL-A SAUCE

- ½ cup mayonnaise
- 2 teaspoons mustard
- 1 teaspoon lemon juice

- 2 tablespoons honey
- 1 tablespoon barbecue sauce

Place all ingredients together in a bowl and stir until completely combined.

DISNEYLAND MONTE CRISTO SANDWICH

Prep time: 15 minutes | Cook time: 30 minutes | Total time: 45 minutes | Makes: 6 servings

Vegetable oil, for frying

6 slices bread

6 slices ham

6 slices provolone cheese

6 slices turkey

6 slices Swiss cheese

1 egg

1 cup all-purpose flour

1 tablespoon baking powder

¼ teaspoon salt

1 tablespoon sugar

1 cup water

Powdered sugar, for topping

Raspberry jam, for dipping

In a large pot or deep fryer, heat 1 to 2 inches vegetable oil to 350 degrees F.

To assemble sandwich, layer one slice of bread, ham, provolone cheese, turkey, and Swiss cheese, and then another slice of bread. Secure all four corners of the sandwich with toothpicks.

In a small bowl, beat the egg. Add flour, baking powder, salt, sugar, and water and mix until smooth. Dip sandwich in batter, coating all edges and sides. Carefully fry sandwich until golden brown (about 2 to 3 minutes) on each side. Remove from oil and place on a paper-towel-lined plate to soak up the extra oil. Sprinkle with powdered sugar, remove toothpicks, and serve with your favorite raspberry jam.

TACO BELL QUESARITO

Prep time: 20 minutes | Cook time: 30 minutes | Total time: 50 minutes | Makes: 4 servings

½ cup cooked rice

2 tablespoons chopped cilantro

1 pound flank steak

Salt and pepper to taste

½ tablespoon olive oil

8 flour tortillas

2 cups shredded cheddar cheese

½ cup nacho cheese

2 tablespoons chipotle salsa

In a small bowl, mix together cooked rice and cilantro. Dice flank steak into bite-size pieces, then salt and pepper to taste.

Heat olive oil in a skillet over medium-high heat. Add steak and cook until it reaches desired doneness. Set aside.

In a large skillet over medium heat, place one tortilla and cover with ½ cup of shredded cheese, then place a second tortilla on top. Cook quesadilla until lightly-browned, about 2 to 3 minutes on each side. Remove and top with ⅛ cup rice mixture, ⅛ cup nacho cheese, ½ tablespoon chipotle salsa, and ¼ of the meat mixture. Tuck in the sides of the tortilla and roll up burrito style. Place seam-side down in the skillet used to make the quesadilla and brown on each side, about 1 to 2 minutes. Repeat process with remaining ingredients and serve warm.

DICKEY'S BARBECUE PIT PULLED PORK SANDWICH

Prep time: 10 minutes | Cook time: 8 hours | Total time: 8 hours 10 minutes | Makes: 8 servings

1 (2½- to 3-pound) pork roast

1 tablespoon Cajun seasoning

1 tablespoon butter

1 yellow onion, chopped

4 teaspoons minced garlic

4 cups water

1 tablespoon liquid smoke

1 teaspoon sea salt

1 cup barbecue sauce

8 hamburger buns

Cut the pork into 4 pieces and place in the slow cooker. Sprinkle Cajun seasoning on all sides of the pork pieces.

Melt the butter in a large skillet over medium heat. Add the chopped onion and minced garlic. Cook over medium heat until onions are slightly tender. Add the water and then pour the mixture over the pork in the slow cooker. Add the liquid smoke and sea salt over the pork. Cook on low 8 hours. Pork will be very tender. Remove from slow cooker and shred with a fork. Place desired amount of pork on a bun and add barbecue sauce.

WINGERS BAR AND GRILL STICKY CHICKEN FINGERS

Prep time: 10 minutes | Cook time: 28 minutes | Total time: 38 minutes | Makes: 6 servings

1 (25-ounce) package frozen breaded chicken strips

6 tablespoons Frank's Hot Sauce

4 tablespoons water

1½ cups brown sugar

Prepare the chicken strips as directed on the back of the package. Heat hot sauce, water, and brown sugar in a saucepan over medium heat until sugar is dissolved. Pour sauce over chicken. Serve with celery and ranch dressing for dipping.

PANERA BREAD ASIAN SESAME CHICKEN SALAD

Prep time: 20 minutes | Cook time: 15 minutes | Total time: 35 minutes | Makes: 4 servings

- 3 tablespoons soy sauce
- 3 teaspoons brown sugar
- 1 teaspoon sesame oil
- ½ teaspoon garlic powder
- ½ teaspoon ground ginger
- 4 boneless, skinless chicken breasts
- 4 cups baby spinach leaves
- 4 cups chopped romaine lettuce

- 1 recipe Asian Dressing
- Fresh cilantro, chopped
- ½ cup sliced almonds
- 1 (11-ounce) can mandarin oranges, drained
- 1 cup wonton strips
- 1 recipe Asian Dressing

In a medium bowl, mix together soy sauce, brown sugar, sesame oil, garlic powder, and ginger. Pour into a gallon-size bag, add chicken breasts, and let marinate in refrigerator for 20 minutes. Make sure to turn every few minutes so all sides of the chicken breast get covered with marinade. Cook on the grill over medium-low heat until cooked through. Make slices in each chicken breast after grilling.

Prepare each plate by placing spinach leaves and romaine lettuce on it. Top off with a grilled chicken breast. Add Asian Dressing and then top each salad off with cilantro, almonds, oranges, and wonton strips.

ASIAN DRESSING

- ½ cup rice vinegar
- ¼ cup sugar
- 2 tablespoons canola oil

- Salt and pepper to taste
- ½ teaspoon toasted sesame seeds

Bring the vinegar to a boil in a small saucepan. Remove from heat, add in the sugar, and stir until dissolved. Cool slightly and then add in the canola oil, salt, pepper, and toasted sesame seeds.

DISNEYLAND CLAM CHOWDER

Prep time: 20 minutes | Cook time: 30 minutes | Total time: 50 minutes | Makes: 8 servings

5 tablespoons butter	1½ cups heavy cream
5 tablespoons all-purpose flour	2¼ cups clam juice
2 tablespoons vegetable oil	1 cup chopped clams
1½ cups diced potatoes	½ tablespoon dried thyme
½ cup diced onion	½ teaspoon salt
½ cup diced red pepper	1 pinch white pepper
½ cup diced green pepper	½ teaspoon Tabasco sauce
½ cup diced celery	

Melt the butter in a large saucepan and then add the flour to make a roux. Cook for 10 minutes over medium heat, stirring often, then set aside.

In a large pot, heat the oil and sauté the potatoes, onion, peppers, and celery over medium heat until the potatoes are just barely tender, about 10 minutes, or until the potatoes are cooked. Add the heavy cream, clam juice, clams, thyme, salt, pepper, Tabasco sauce, and roux. Whisk well to blend in the roux. Bring to a boil, then reduce the heat and simmer for about 5 minutes, stirring occasionally. Add more seasoning to taste.

THE CHEESECAKE FACTORY CHICKEN MADEIRA

Prep time: 40 minutes | Cook time: 40 minutes | Total time: 1 hour 20 minutes | Makes: 4 servings

- **4 boneless, skinless chicken breasts, pounded to ¼-inch thick**
- **1¼ cups balsamic vinaigrette, divided**
- **4 tablespoons brown sugar, divided**
- **2 tablespoons olive oil**
- **2 tablespoons butter**

- **2 cups sliced white mushrooms**
- **2 cups beef stock**
- **1 cup shredded mozzarella cheese**
- **Fresh parsley, for garnishing**

Place chicken, 1 cup balsamic vinaigrette, and 2 tablespoons brown sugar in a large zipper top bag. Seal and shake well to coat chicken. Marinate in refrigerator at least 30 minutes.

Preheat oven to 350 degrees F.

Heat oil in a large skillet over medium-high heat. Remove chicken from bag and cook in hot oil 4 to 6 minutes on each side, until chicken is golden brown. Once browned, remove chicken and place in an oven-safe dish. Bake 10 to 15 minutes, until chicken is cooked through.

In the same skillet used for cooking the chicken, melt butter over medium heat. Add mushrooms and sauté 2 to 3 minutes. Add ¼ cup balsamic vinaigrette, 2 tablespoons brown sugar, and beef stock and bring to a boil. Reduce heat and simmer 20 to 25 minutes, until the sauce has been reduced by about 50 percent.

Top cooked chicken with mozzarella cheese and broil 3 to 4 minutes, until the cheese starts to turn golden brown. Serve chicken immediately with sauce poured over top.

RED LOBSTER SHRIMP LINGUINE

Prep time: 10 minutes | Cook time: 15 minutes | Total time: 25 minutes | Makes: 4 servings

8   ounces linguine

2   tablespoons olive oil

3   teaspoons minced garlic

1½ pounds baby shrimp, peeled and deveined

¼   cup butter

3   tablespoons all-purpose flour

1   (8-ounce) package cream cheese

½   cup grated Parmesan cheese

¼   cup white wine vinegar

¼   cup half and half

Chives to taste

Salt and pepper to taste

Cook linguine according to package directions and set aside. Heat oil in a large skillet over medium heat. Add garlic and cook until fragrant, about 30 seconds. Add shrimp and cook until it turns pink and tender, about 3 to 4 minutes. Once cooked, remove shrimp and set aside.

Add butter to the hot skillet and let it melt. Slowly whisk in flour until fully incorporated. Add in cream cheese, whisking until smooth. Add in Parmesan cheese, white wine vinegar, and half and half. Add more or less half and half to reach your desired consistency. Add cooked linguine and shrimp back to the skillet. Stir to combine. Top with chives, salt, and pepper to taste.

PANDA EXPRESS ORANGE CHICKEN

Prep time: 15 minutes | Cook time: 15 minutes | Total time: 30 minutes | Makes: 6 servings

- 2 pounds boneless, skinless chicken breasts
- 1 egg
- 1½ teaspoons salt
- ¼ teaspoon ground black pepper
- 1 tablespoon vegetable oil, plus more for frying

- ½ cup cornstarch
- ¼ cup all-purpose flour
- 1 (12.5-ounce) bottle orange sauce, such as Panda Express Gourmet Chinese Orange sauce

Cut chicken breasts into bite-size pieces, trimming off any fat. Pour oil an inch deep in a cast-iron pot or saucepan and heat over medium-high heat. In a medium bowl, whisk together egg, salt, pepper, and vegetable oil. In another bowl, mix together cornstarch and flour. Coat the chicken in the egg mixture, then dredge in the flour mixture. Add coated chicken to the heated oil (you may need to do this in a few batches). Cook each side for at least 2 to 3 minutes or until golden brown and chicken is cooked through. Place chicken on paper towels to soak up any oil.

In a large bowl, toss together cooked chicken and orange sauce. Serve warm with rice or our Panda Express Chow Mein (see recipe on page 15).

OLIVE GARDEN CHICKEN PARMESAN

Prep time: 10 minutes | Cook time: 25 minutes | Total time: 35 minutes | Makes: 4 servings

2 **cups croutons**

4 **boneless, skinless chicken breasts**

1 **egg, beaten**

1 **cup marinara sauce**

½ **cup shredded mozzarella cheese**

Preheat oven to 375 degrees F. Spray a 9x13-inch baking dish with nonstick cooking spray.

In a food processor (or in a zipper-top bag using a rolling pin), crush croutons into fine crumbs. Place in a shallow dish or container. Dip each chicken breast in egg, then dredge through crouton crumbs. Place coated chicken in prepared baking dish. Bake 20 to 30 minutes, until chicken is cooked through. Remove from oven and evenly distribute marinara sauce over each chicken breast. Top each chicken breast evenly with mozzarella cheese. Heat oven to broil. Return chicken to oven and cook until sauce is warm and cheese starts to bubble and brown, about 3 to 4 minutes.

OLIVE GARDEN ZUPPA TOSCANA

Prep time: 15 minutes | Cook time: 30 minutes | Total time: 45 minutes | Makes: 6 servings

- 1 pound Italian sausage, casings removed
- 4 slices thick bacon, diced into small pieces
- 1 large sweet onion, chopped
- 3 large potatoes
- 4 cups low-sodium chicken broth
- 2 cups water

- 2 garlic cloves, minced
- ¼ teaspoon crushed red pepper flakes
  Salt and pepper to taste
- 2 cups chopped kale, packed
- 1½ cups half and half
  Finely shredded Parmesan cheese, for garnish

Crumble sausage into 1-inch pieces and add to a large saucepan over medium high heat. Cook sausage, stirring occasionally, until cooked through. Drain sausage onto a plate or baking dish lined with paper towels; set aside.

Add diced bacon and chopped onion to saucepan and sauté mixture until bacon is cooked through and onions are translucent, about 3 to 5 minutes longer.

Scrub and rinse potatoes, then slice into halves. Slice halves into ¼-inch slices. Add chicken broth, water, sliced potatoes, garlic, red pepper flakes, and salt and pepper to saucepan with bacon and onions. Bring soup just to a boil, then reduce heat to medium-low and stir in cooked sausage. Cover saucepan and simmer, stirring occasionally, until potatoes are nearly tender, about 10 to 15 minutes. Add in kale, then simmer until potatoes are soft and kale is tender, about 5 to 10 minutes longer. Stir in half and half and warm through.

Serve warm topped with Parmesan cheese.

CHILI'S CAJUN CHICKEN PASTA

Prep time: 10 minutes | Cook time: 20 minutes | Total time: 30 minutes | Makes: 4 servings

8   ounces penne pasta

2   boneless, skinless chicken breasts

4   teaspoons Cajun seasoning

4   tablespoons butter, divided

3   cups half and half

½   teaspoon lemon pepper seasoning

1   teaspoon salt

1   teaspoon ground black pepper

¼   teaspoon garlic powder

2   tomatoes, diced

½   cup shredded Parmesan cheese

Cook penne pasta according to directions on the box. Drain pasta and set aside.

Place chicken breasts in a zipper-top plastic bag and sprinkle in Cajun seasoning. Seal bag and shake thoroughly until chicken is evenly coated.

In a large skillet, sauté chicken breasts in 2 tablespoons butter over medium heat, turning occasionally until cooked through.

In a separate skillet, combine half and half, 2 tablespoons butter, lemon pepper, salt, black pepper, and garlic powder over medium heat, stirring occasionally. Remove from heat when cream mixture starts to bubble.

Pour cream sauce over cooked noodles. Slice chicken breasts into strips. Serve pasta on serving plates, topped with chicken-breast strips, diced tomatoes, and Parmesan cheese.

OLIVE GARDEN GRILLED CHICKEN FLATBREAD PIZZA

Prep time: 10 minutes | Cook time: 7 minutes | Total time: 17 minutes | Makes: 4 servings

1   red pepper

4   (6- to 8-inch) pieces flatbread, such as pita bread

1   cup jarred Alfredo sauce

2   cups shredded mozzarella cheese

2   chicken breasts, grilled and thinly sliced

1   Roma tomato, diced

3   green onions, thinly sliced

Preheat the oven broiler.

Slice red pepper and lightly coat with olive oil. Line a baking sheet with foil and lay pepper slices in a single layer on the sheet. Roast peppers under the broiler until the skin starts to turn dark, about 4 to 5 minutes; watch carefully so they don't burn. Set aside once roasted.

Preheat oven to 350 degrees F.

Place the flatbread on a large baking sheet. Spread Alfredo sauce on each flatbread, then top with cheese, chicken, roasted peppers, tomatoes, and green onions. Place in the oven and cook 5 to 7 minutes, or until cheese melts.

BLUE LEMON PINEAPPLE BBQ BEEF SANDWICH

Prep time: 10 minutes | Cook time: 5 hours | Total time: 5 hours 10 minutes | Makes: 8 servings

1 (2- to 3-pound) beef rump roast

1 (20-ounce) can pineapple chunks, juice reserved

1 onion, diced

½ cup apple cider vinegar

⅓ cup brown sugar

½ cup ketchup

1 tablespoon Dijon mustard

2 tablespoons Worcestershire sauce

8 hamburger buns

Spray slow cooker insert with nonstick cooking spray. Place roast inside.

In a separate bowl, mix together juice from pineapple, onion, vinegar, brown sugar, ketchup, mustard, and Worcestershire sauce. Pour over roast.

Add pineapple chunks to roast and cook on low 10 hours or high for 5 to 6 hours.

When finished, shred meat using two forks (it should just fall apart by this time). Serve meat on toasted buns, topped with your favorite sandwich fixings, such as red onions, lettuce, tomatoes, and cheese.

McDONALD'S BIG MAC

Prep time: 15 minutes | Cook time: 10 minutes | Total time: 25 minutes | Makes: 4 servings

2 pounds ground beef, split into 8 patties

Salt and pepper to taste

4 sesame seed hamburger buns

4 additional bottom halves of hamburger buns

Shredded lettuce

16 dill pickle slices

8 slices cheddar cheese

1 recipe McDonald's Special Sauce

Preheat grill over medium-high heat. Season patties with salt and pepper and cook over direct heat 3 to 5 minutes per side. Remove patties from grill.

Assemble burgers, starting from the bottom: bottom bun, McDonald's Special Sauce, shredded lettuce, hamburger patty, two dill pickles, slice of cheese, additional bottom bun, McDonald's Special Sauce, shredded lettuce, hamburger patty, two dill pickles, top bun.

McDONALD'S SPECIAL SAUCE

½ cup mayonnaise

2 tablespoons French dressing

4 teaspoons sweet pickle relish

1 tablespoon minced white onion

1 teaspoon white vinegar

1 teaspoon sugar

⅛ teaspoon salt

Mix all ingredients together until combined well; chill in refrigerator until ready to use.

IN-N-OUT BURGER

Prep time: 15 minutes | Cook time: 10 minutes | Total time: 25 minutes | Makes: 4 servings

- 1 pound 80/20 ground beef
- 1 teaspoon kosher salt
- ¼ teaspoon ground black pepper
- 4 slices cheddar cheese
- 4 hamburger buns, lightly toasted
- 1 large beefsteak tomato, thinly sliced into 8 slices
- 4 large iceberg lettuce leaves
- 1 small onion, thickly sliced
- 1 recipe In-N-Out Sauce

In a large bowl, mix together ground beef, salt, and pepper with your hands. Form the meat into 4 thin patties, each about ½-inch thick.

Heat grill over medium-high heat. Place patties on grill and cook about 3 to 4 minutes. Flip each burger patty and top with a slice of cheese, if desired. Cook until the cheese begins to droop and melt at the corners and edges.

While the burgers cook, slather the bottom half of each bun with about 1 tablespoon In-N-Out Sauce. To build each burger, top the In-N-Out Sauce with 2 tomato slices, 1 lettuce leaf, the cooked burger, 1 slice onion, and finish with the top bun. Serve immediately.

IN-N-OUT SAUCE

- ¼ cup mayonnaise
- 2 tablespoons ketchup
- 1 tablespoon sweet pickle relish
- ¼ teaspoon Worcestershire sauce

Stir together the mayonnaise, ketchup, relish, and Worcestershire sauce in a small bowl. Refrigerate until ready to use.

FAMOUS DAVE'S BBQ RIBS

Prep time: 50 minutes, plus marinating time overnight | Cook time: 7½ hours | Total time: 8 hours 20 minutes, plus marinating time overnight | Makes: 6 servings

- 10 pounds ribs
- ½ cup Italian salad dressing
- ½ teaspoon ground black pepper
- 1 tablespoon brown sugar
- ¼ cup minced dry onion
- 1 recipe Rib Rub
- 1 (16-ounce) bottle Famous Dave's BBQ sauce

The day before smoking the ribs, trim all excess fat from the ribs. Place ribs in a large zipper-top plastic bag. Pour in Italian dressing and turn bag over several times to coat all meat. Seal well and marinate in refrigerator 4 to 6 hours, turning occasionally.

Remove meat and wipe excess dressing off. Sprinkle each rib with pepper, 1 tablespoon brown sugar, and dried onion. Wrap each rib in plastic wrap and refrigerate overnight.

The next morning, remove ribs from wrap and wipe marinade off the meat. Generously coat both front and back of ribs with Rib Rub. Using your hands; rub seasoning into meat and set aside.

Place ribs on smoker and smoke for six hours, following the smoker's directions.

Remove ribs from smoker and wrap in aluminum foil. Place on grill preheated to medium-low heat, add BBQ sauce, and let cook 1½ hours or until ribs are fork tender and the meat has started to pull away from the bones. Top with extra BBQ sauce, if desired.

Serve immediately.

RIB RUB

- ½ cup packed brown sugar
- 1 tablespoon salt
- 1 tablespoon sugar
- 1 teaspoon garlic powder
- ½ teaspoon chili powder
- ½ teaspoon onion salt
- ½ teaspoon celery salt
- ½ teaspoon lemon pepper
- ¼ teaspoon ground black pepper

Combine all ingredients in a small bowl and store in airtight container until ready to use.

NOODLES & COMPANY PESTO CAVATAPPI

Prep time: 10 minutes | Cook time: 15 minutes | Total time: 25 minutes | Makes: 4 servings

15 to 20 **basil leaves**

½ **cup grated Parmesan cheese, plus more for topping**

½ **teaspoon salt**

2 **cloves garlic**

2 **tablespoons olive oil, divided**

8 **ounces Cavatappi noodles**

1 **cup sliced mushrooms**

1 **cup sliced cherry tomatoes**

½ **teaspoon garlic salt**

¼ **cup milk**

Rinse basil leaves in cold water.

In a food processor or high-powered blender, combine basil leaves, ½ cup Parmesan cheese, salt, garlic, and 1½ tablespoons olive oil. It will create a paste-like sauce (if it is too thick, add a little milk to the sauce); set aside.

Cook pasta according to the directions on the box.

While the noodles are cooking, sauté mushrooms with ½ tablespoon olive oil over medium heat.

After about 3 minutes, add sliced cherry tomatoes along with garlic salt and let them cook together about 8 minutes, stirring occasionally.

Drain noodles. Reduce heat on tomatoes and mushrooms to low, and add noodles to the sauté pan. Add pesto sauce and stir well. Once everything is mixed together, add about ¼ cup of milk to the mixture. You can add more or less depending on how thick you like your sauce.

Top with grated Parmesan cheese.

CRACKER BARREL HASH BROWN CASSEROLE

Prep time: 10 minutes | Cook time: 50 minutes | Total time: 1 hour | Makes: 8 servings

- 1 **(30-ounce) bag frozen hash browns, thawed**
- ½ **cup butter, melted**
- 1 **(14.5-ounce) can cream of chicken soup**
- 1 **small yellow onion, chopped**

- 2 **cups shredded cheddar cheese**
- 1 **teaspoon salt**
- ½ **teaspoon ground black pepper**
- 1 **cup sour cream**

Preheat oven to 350 degrees F. Grease a 9×13-inch baking dish.

In a large bowl, combine hash browns, butter, cream of chicken soup, onion, 1 cup of the cheese, salt, pepper, and sour cream. Transfer to prepared baking dish and bake 45 minutes, until cheese has melted and hash browns begin to golden.

Remove from oven and top with remaining cheese. Cook an additional 5 minutes, or until cheese begins to bubble.

PANERA BREAD MAC & CHEESE

Prep time: 5 minutes | Cook time: 15 minutes | Total time: 20 minutes | Makes: 6 servings

1 (16-ounce) package elbow macaroni

¼ cup butter

¼ cup all-purpose flour

2 cups milk

6 slices white American cheese

2 cups shredded extra-sharp white cheddar

½ teaspoon Dijon mustard

1 teaspoon salt

½ teaspoon ground black pepper

¼ teaspoon hot sauce

Prepare pasta according package directions; set aside.

In a large saucepan over medium heat, melt butter. Whisk in flour and cook for 1 minute.

Slowly whisk in milk and continue stirring over medium heat until mixture thickens and begins to bubble.

Remove from heat and mix In cheeses, mustard, salt, pepper, and hot sauce. Stir until cheese has completely melted and mixture is smooth.

Stir in pasta and cook over medium heat for one more minute, or until mixture is heated through.

HABIT BURGER CHICKEN CLUB SANDWICH

Prep time: 35 minutes | Cook time: 10 minutes | Total time: 35 minutes | Makes: 6 servings

6 boneless, skinless chicken breasts	12 slices sourdough bread
¼ cup olive oil	3 avocados, mashed
2 tablespoons honey	2 tablespoons mayonnaise
2 tablespoons lime juice	12 strips bacon, cooked crisp
½ teaspoon chili powder	1 tomato, sliced
¼ teaspoon cumin	Lettuce for topping

Mix oil, honey, lime juice, chili powder, and cumin in a large zipper top bag. Place chicken inside, seal bag, and massage bag so that chicken is fully coated by marinade. Refrigerate at least 30 minutes.

Remove chicken from fridge and preheat grill to medium-high heat. Grill the chicken for 2 to 3 minutes on each side, turning once, until the chicken is no longer pink and reaches an internal temperature of 165 degrees F.

Toast bread in a toaster or under the broiler of an oven.

To assemble sandwich, layer mayonnaise, mashed avocado, bacon, tomato, lettuce, and grilled chicken on bread. Top with another slice of bread.

CHILI'S ENCHILADA SOUP

Prep time: 15 minutes | Cook time: 45 minutes | Total time: 1 hour | Makes: 6 servings

2 **tablespoons olive oil**	1 **teaspoon onion powder**
2 **teaspoons minced garlic**	½ **teaspoon ground black pepper**
½ **cup diced onion**	½ **teaspoon cumin**
1 **cup masa harina (corn tortilla flour)**	3 **boneless, skinless chicken breasts, cooked and shredded**
2 **(14.5-ounce) cans chicken broth**	
4 **cups water**	2 **cups shredded cheddar cheese**
1 **cup enchilada sauce**	**Corn tortilla chips**
1 **teaspoon salt**	

Heat a large pot or Dutch oven over medium-high heat. Add olive oil and allow it to heat through. Add garlic and onion. Cook until the onions are translucent and a bit golden, about 10 minutes.

Add masa harina to the onion mixture and cook and stir for 1 to 2 minutes.

Slowly stir in chicken broth until combined and smooth.

Mix in water, enchilada sauce, salt, onion powder, pepper, cumin, and chicken.

Cover and simmer 20 minutes.

Mix in cheese until completely melted. Serve with tortilla chips.

PANERA BREAD BROCCOLI CHEDDAR SOUP

Prep time: 10 minutes | Cook time: 25 minutes | Total time: 35 minutes | Makes: 6 servings

- 1 tablespoon butter, melted
- ½ medium onion, chopped
- ¼ cup butter, melted
- ½ cup all-purpose flour
- 2 cups half and half
- 2 cups chicken stock
- 3 cups chopped, fresh broccoli

- 1 cup julienned carrots (or packaged matchstick carrots from the produce section)
- Salt and pepper to taste
- 2 cups shredded sharp cheddar cheese
- ¼ teaspoon ground nutmeg

In a small skillet over medium heat, melt 1 tablespoon butter. Add onion and sauté until translucent, about 9 minutes; set aside.

In a large saucepan over medium heat, whisk together the ¼ cup melted butter and flour; cook and stir 2 to 3 minutes, until nutty brown and fragrant. Whisk in the half and half and chicken stock, reduce heat, and simmer 10 minutes, stirring occasionally.

Add the broccoli, carrots, and sautéed onions. Cook over low heat 20 to 25 minutes.

Add salt and pepper. Scoop out about 1 cup of the soup and puree in blender. Add pureed soup back to saucepan. Stir in cheese and nutmeg over low heat until cheese melts. Don't set temperature any higher than this, or the soup may take on a grainy texture.

MACARONI GRILL PENNE RUSTICA

Prep time: 25 minutes | Cook time: 10 to 15 minutes | Total time: 35 to 40 minutes | Makes: 10 servings

1 teaspoon butter	24 precooked shrimp, peeled and deveined
1 teaspoon chopped garlic	2 large chicken breasts, cooked and chopped
½ teaspoon chopped rosemary	8 to 12 ounces penne pasta, cooked
½ teaspoon Dijon mustard	½ teaspoon chopped green onions
½ teaspoon garlic salt	Pinch salt and pepper
4 cups heavy cream	½ cup grated Parmesan cheese
1 (8-ounce) package cream cheese	¼ teaspoon paprika
½ cup bacon bits	

Preheat oven to 475 degrees F.

In a skillet over medium heat, melt butter. Add garlic and rosemary and sauté briefly, until garlic begins to brown. Quickly add Dijon mustard, garlic salt, heavy cream, and cream cheese. Stir until cream cheese melts and mixture is combined and bubbly; set aside while assembling pasta.

In a 9x13-inch baking pan, add bacon, shrimp, chicken, pasta, green onions, salt, and pepper, tossing to combine well. Pour sauce over top and then sprinkle with Parmesan cheese and paprika.

Bake 10 to 15 minutes, until golden brown and bubbly.

KNEADERS CHICKEN BACON AVOCADO SANDWICH

Prep time: 10 minutes | Makes: 2 servings

1 recipe Kneaders Sauce (see recipe below)

2 slices provolone cheese

1 chicken breast, cut into strips

4 strips bacon, cooked crisp

2 large lettuce leaves

4 to 6 slices tomato

¼ small red onion, thinly sliced

1 avocado, peeled, pitted, and sliced
Salt and pepper to taste

4 slices bread, such as focaccia or a hearty white bread

Spread Kneaders Sauce lightly on each slice of bread. Then layer half of the cheese, chicken, bacon, lettuce, tomato, onion, avocado, and sprinkle salt and pepper on one slice of bread. Top with a second slice of bread, placing bread sauce-side down. Repeat with remaining bread and the other half of the sandwich toppings.

KNEADERS SAUCE

½ cup mayonnaise

2 tablespoons sour cream

2 teaspoons yellow mustard

In a small bowl, stir together mayonnaise, sour cream, and mustard. Cover and refrigerate until ready to use.

APPLEBEE'S HONEY GRILLED SALMON

Prep time: 10 minutes | Cook time: 20 minutes | Total time: 30 minutes | Makes: 4 servings

¾ cup honey

⅓ cup soy sauce

¼ cup packed dark brown sugar

¼ cup pineapple juice

2 tablespoons fresh lemon juice

2 tablespoons distilled white vinegar

2 teaspoons olive oil

1 teaspoon ground black pepper

½ teaspoon cayenne pepper

½ teaspoon paprika

¼ teaspoon garlic powder

Vegetable oil

4 (8-ounce) salmon fillets, skin removed

Salt and pepper to taste

In a medium saucepan over medium-low heat, whisk together the honey, soy sauce, brown sugar, pineapple juice, lemon juice, vinegar, olive oil, pepper, cayenne pepper, paprika, and garlic powder. Cook, stirring occasionally, until sauce begins to boil. Reduce heat and simmer uncovered 10 to 15 minutes, or until syrupy.

Preheat grill to medium heat. Rub each salmon filet with vegetable oil, then add a light sprinkling of salt and pepper.

Grill the salmon 4 to 7 minutes per side, or until done.

Serve salmon with a small cup of the honey-pepper sauce on the side.

BONEFISH GRILL BANG BANG SHRIMP

Prep time: 10 minutes | Cook time: 10 minutes | Total time: 20 minutes | Makes: 4 servings

½ cup mayonnaise

¼ cup Thai sweet chili sauce

¼ teaspoon Sriracha

1 pound shrimp, shelled and deveined

½ cup buttermilk

¾ cup cornstarch

Canola oil, for frying

In a small bowl, whisk together the mayonnaise, Thai sweet chili sauce, and Sriracha.

In a separate medium bowl, add the shrimp and the buttermilk and stir to completely cover the shrimp with milk. Place cornstarch in a separate shallow bowl. Remove the shrimp from the buttermilk and dredge in the cornstarch.

In a heavy-bottomed pan, add 2 to 3 inches canola oil and heat oil to 375 degrees F. Fry the shrimp until lightly brown, about 1 minute on each side.

Once they are lightly fried, place shrimp on a paper towel-lined pan to soak up any extra oil. Put shrimp in a bowl and pour the sauce over top of it. Toss to coat and serve.

CAFE RIO STEAK SALAD

Prep time: 2 hours 15 minutes | Cook time: 45 minutes | Total time: 3 hours | Makes: 4 to 6 servings

4 to 6 flour tortillas

1 cup Cilantro Lime Rice

2 cups Black Beans

2 pounds Cafe Rio Steak

1 bunch romaine lettuce, chopped

1 cup Pico de Gallo

1 cup Guacamole

½ cup sour cream, for topping

2 tablespoons grated Parmesan or cotija cheese, for topping

1 cup tortilla strips, for topping

¼ cup chopped cilantro, for topping

1 recipe Cilantro Ranch Dressing

Place one flour tortilla and on the bottom of a bowl or plate.

Top with Cilantro Lime Rice, followed by the Black Beans, and then the Cafe Rio Steak.

Add romaine lettuce. Top with a scoop of Pico de Gallo, a scoop Guacamole, and a dollop of sour cream.

Sprinkle with Parmesan or cotija cheese, tortilla strips, and cilantro.

Serve with Cilantro Ranch Dressing.

CILANTRO LIME RICE

Prep time: 10 minutes | Cook time: 25 minutes | Total time: 35 minutes | Makes: 4 to 6 servings

1 cup uncooked rice

1 teaspoon butter or margarine

2 teaspoons minced garlic

1 teaspoon freshly squeezed lime juice

1 (15-ounce) can chicken broth

1 cup water

1 tablespoon freshly squeezed lime juice

2 teaspoons sugar

3 tablespoons fresh, chopped cilantro

In a medium saucepan, combine rice, butter, garlic, 1 teaspoon lime juice, chicken broth, and water. Bring to a boil. Cover and cook on low heat, 15 to 20 minutes, until rice is tender. Remove from heat.

In a small bowl, combine 1 tablespoon lime juice, sugar, and cilantro. Pour over hot cooked rice and mix in as you fluff the rice.

BLACK BEANS

Prep time: 5 minutes | Cook time: 10 minutes | Total time: 15 minutes | Makes: 4 to 6 servings

2	tablespoons olive oil	1	cup tomato juice
2	teaspoons minced garlic	1½	teaspoons salt
1	teaspoon ground cumin	2	tablespoons fresh chopped cilantro
1	(15-ounce) can black beans, rinsed and drained		

Heat oil in a nonstick skillet, over medium heat until shiny but not smoking. Add garlic and cumin and cook until fragrant, about 30 seconds. Add beans, tomato juice, and salt. Stir continuously until heated through. Just before serving, stir in the cilantro.

CAFE RIO STEAK

Prep time: 40 minutes | Cook time: 10 minutes | Total time: 50 minutes | Makes: 4 to 6 servings

¼	cup honey	1	teaspoon minced garlic
¼	cup soy sauce	2	pounds skirt or flank steak, sliced into ½-inch thick slices across the grain
2	tablespoons lemon juice		
½	teaspoon ground ginger		

In a medium zipper-top bag, add honey, soy sauce, lemon juice, ginger, and garlic. Add steak, seal bag tightly, and shake or massage bag to mix marinade and coat the steaks. Marinate at least 30 minutes in the refrigerator. (You can also marinate overnight if desired; the longer steak marinates, the stronger the flavor.)

Heat grill to medium. Remove steak from marinade and discard marinade. Grill steak 3 to 4 minutes on each side, until strips reach desired doneness.

PICO DE GALLO

Prep time: 40 minutes | Total time: 40 minutes | Makes: 4 to 6 servings

2 medium tomatoes, diced	1 to 2 cloves garlic, freshly minced
1 red onion, finely chopped	2 to 3 sprigs fresh cilantro, finely chopped
1 green onion, finely chopped	Juice of one lime
½ jalapeño, seeded and chopped	Salt and pepper to taste

In a small bowl, combine tomatoes, onions, jalapeño, garlic, and cilantro. Sprinkle with lime juice and season with salt and pepper to taste. Toss well and refrigerate at least 30 minutes before serving.

GUACAMOLE

Prep time: 40 minutes | Total time: 40 minutes | Makes: 4 to 6 servings

2 avocados	1 ripe tomato, chopped
1 small onion, finely chopped	Juice of 1 lime
1 teaspoon minced garlic	Salt and pepper to taste

Peel and mash avocados in a medium serving bowl. Stir in onion, garlic, tomato, lime juice, salt, and pepper. Season with any remaining lime juice and salt and pepper to taste. Chill, tightly covered with plastic wrap, for 30 minutes to blend flavors.

CILANTRO RANCH DRESSING

Prep time: 5 minutes | Total time: 5 minutes | Makes: 4 to 6 servings

1 packet traditional Hidden Valley Ranch dressing mix (not the buttermilk variety)	2 tomatillos, husks removed and diced
	½ bunch fresh cilantro, chopped
1 cup mayonnaise	1 teaspoon minced garlic
1 cup buttermilk	Juice of 1 lime
	1 jalapeño, seeded and diced

Mix all ingredients together in a blender until smooth and well combined.

BAJIO MEXICAN GRILL SLOW COOKER CHICKEN TACOS

Prep time: 10 minutes | Cook time: 6 hours | Total time: 6 hours 10 minutes | Makes: 8 servings

5   boneless skinless chicken breasts

½   cup salsa

1   tablespoon ground cumin

½   cup brown sugar, or more, to taste

1   (4-ounce) can diced green chilies

¾   cup lemon-lime soda (half a 12-ounce can)

8   flour tortillas

Lettuce, avocado, diced tomatoes, black beans, shredded cheese, and other taco toppings as desired

Place chicken breasts in slow cooker. In a small bowl, combine salsa, cumin, brown sugar, and green chilies. Mix well and pour over chicken. Pour lemon-lime soda over all. Cover and cook on low 5 to 6 hours.

Remove chicken and shred. Return to slow cooker and cook 1 more hour. If desired, thicken the juices with a little cornstarch mixed in water.

Serve shredded meat in flour tortillas with lettuce, cheese, black beans, and any other taco fixings.

Note: If you like a spicier taco, use a hotter salsa and more green chilies and reduce the amount of brown sugar.

BONEFISH GRILL FISH TACOS

Prep time: 10 minutes | Cook time: 10 minutes | Total time: 20 minutes | Makes: 4 servings

1 pound flaky white fish, such as catfish or cod

4 tablespoons fresh lime juice

2 tablespoons vegetable oil

2 tablespoons soy sauce

1 recipe Bonefish Special Sauce

1 recipe Mango Salsa

10 to 12 corn tortillas

3 cups shredded slaw mix (red and green cabbage, carrots)

Combine fresh lime juice with the vegetable oil and soy sauce in a 9x13-inch baking dish. Add the fish and turn to coat so pieces are covered in the marinade. Set aside and let marinate while you prepare the rest of the dish.

Remove fish from the marinade and grill or sauté over medium heat until cooked through, about 5 minutes per side.

Stack the tortillas on a plate and cover with a paper towel. Warm in the microwave at high power for 1 minute. To assemble tacos, place fish in a tortilla, and top with shredded slaw mix, Bonefish Special Sauce, and Mango Salsa.

BONEFISH SPECIAL SAUCE

⅓ cup mayonnaise

⅓ cup lowfat yogurt

⅓ cup light sour cream

2 tablespoons fresh lime juice

1 chipotle chili in adobo sauce, finely chopped

1 clove garlic, finely chopped or pressed

Salt to taste

Mix together the mayonnaise, yogurt, sour cream, lime juice, chipotle chili, and chopped garlic in a bowl. Season to taste with salt.

MANGO SALSA

2 red, yellow, and/or orange bell peppers, diced

1 jalapeño pepper, seeded and diced

1 small red onion, finely chopped

3 just-ripe mangoes, peeled and
chopped.

1 bunch cilantro, washed, dried, de-
stemmed, and chopped

2 cloves garlic, minced

Juice of 1 lime

Salt to taste

In a large bowl, toss together the peppers, onions, mangoes, cilantro, garlic, and lime juice. Season to taste with salt.

COPYCAT

Desserts

DISNEYLAND SNICKERDOODLES

Prep time: 15 minutes | Cook time: 8 minutes | Total time: 23 minutes | Makes: 60 cookies

3½ cups all-purpose flour

½ teaspoon baking soda

½ teaspoon cream of tartar

1 cup butter, room temperature

2 cups sugar, plus 3 tablespoons for topping

2 eggs

¼ cup milk

1 teaspoon vanilla

1 teaspoon ground cinnamon

Preheat oven to 375 degrees F.

In a large bowl, sift together flour, baking soda, and cream of tartar. Set aside.

In a separate bowl, cream together the butter and 2 cups sugar with an electric mixer until light and fluffy. Add the eggs, milk, and vanilla. Mix well. Add the wet ingredients to the dry ingredients and mix until everything is incorporated.

In another small bowl, mix together cinnamon and 3 tablespoons sugar for the topping. Form the dough into 1-inch balls and roll in the cinnamon-sugar mixture. Place dough ball on a greased baking sheet and flatten lightly with the bottom of a glass. Sprinkle the tops of the cookies with additional cinnamon sugar mixture, then bake for 7 to 8 minutes. Do not overbake these. Remove from oven and let cool on the cookie sheet for 1 to 2 minutes, then remove to a wire rack to cool.

BJ'S BREWHOUSE PIZZOOKIE

Prep time: 10 minutes | Cook time: 10 minutes | Total time: 20 minutes | Makes: 4 servings

½ **cup unsalted butter, softened**

½ **cup granulated sugar**

½ **cup packed brown sugar**

½ **tablespoon vanilla extract**

1 **large egg**

1½ **cups all-purpose flour**

½ **teaspoon baking soda**

½ **teaspoon salt**

1 **cup milk chocolate chips**

4 **large scoops chocolate chip ice cream**

Chocolate sauce, for topping

Preheat oven to 350 degrees F.

In a medium bowl, cream together butter and sugars until combined. Add in vanilla and egg. Slowly stir in the flour, baking soda, and salt, then fold in chocolate chips. Press the cookie dough mixture into the bottom of an 8-inch cast-iron skillet. Bake 8 to 10 minutes (it will be gooey). Pull out of the oven and top with ice cream, then drizzle with chocolate sauce. Serve while still warm (and before the ice cream melts!).

Note: Change up your chocolate chips and chocolate chip ice cream for other favorite cookie additions and ice cream flavors. We like a cookie with toffee chips and pralines and cream ice cream, or M&M's and chocolate-peanut butter ice cream!

THE CHEESECAKE FACTORY OREO DREAM CHEESECAKE

Prep time: 20 minutes | Cook time: 1 hour, plus 5 for cooling and chilling | Total time: 6 hours 20 minutes | Makes: 8 to 10 servings

- 1 recipe Oreo Cheesecake Crust
- 3 (8-ounce) packages cream cheese, room temperature
- ¼ cup butter, melted
- 1 cup sugar
- 5 large eggs, room temperature

- 2½ teaspoons vanilla extract
- ½ teaspoon salt
- ¼ cup all-purpose flour
- 1 (8-ounce) container sour cream, room temperature
- 18 Oreo cookies, crushed and divided

Preheat oven to 325 degrees F.

In a large bowl, beat cream cheese with an electric mixer until smooth and fluffy. Mix in the ¼ cup melted butter. Slowly beat in sugar, making sure mixture is very smooth. Beat in the eggs one at a time. Add the vanilla, salt, and flour and continue beating until batter is smooth, without any lumps. Add the sour cream and continue to beat. Fold in just over half of the crushed Oreo cookies.

Pour the batter into the pan with the Oreo crust. Garnish top with remaining crushed Oreos. Place in oven and bake 1 hour or until the middle doesn't jiggle. Turn off the oven but do no remove the cheesecake. Prop open the oven door and let cheesecake cool in oven for 1 hour. Refrigerate at least 4 hours, but 24 hours is preferred. Top with whipped cream when ready to serve.

OREO CHEESECAKE CRUST

- 1½ cups crushed Oreo Cookies (about 18 cookies)

- 4 tablespoons butter, melted

Combine Oreo crumbs and butter in a small bowl; press into the bottom and 1½ inches up the sides of a 9-inch springform pan.

KNEADERS RASPBERRY BREAD PUDDING

Prep time: 30 minutes | Cook time: 40 minutes | Total time: 1 hour 10 minutes | Makes: 8 to 10 servings

4 cups heavy cream	5 cups frozen raspberries
3 cups sugar	1 cup sugar
1 egg	½ cup apple juice
1 teaspoon vanilla extract	1 recipe Vanilla Cream Sauce
1½ loaves white bread	

Preheat oven to 375 degrees F.

In a large bowl, combine cream, sugar, egg, and vanilla and beat with an electric mixer until combined well. Cut bread into 1½-inch cubes and fold into cream mixture, until bread is well coated. Let bread sit in cream mixture for 30 minutes, stirring every 5 minutes to allow bread to absorb cream. After 30 minutes, gently fold in raspberries, sugar, and apple juice until well combined and sugar is dissolved. Spread bread mixture in a 9x13-inch baking pan sprayed with nonstick cooking spray. Bake 40 minutes. Serve with warm Vanilla Cream Sauce over top.

VANILLA CREAM SAUCE

1⅓ cups butter	3 cups heavy cream
5 tablespoons flour	⅔ cup sugar
½ teaspoon salt	2 teaspoons vanilla

Melt butter in a medium saucepan over medium heat. Add flour and whisk constantly for 10 minutes, being sure not to let the butter brown. Add salt, cream, and sugar and stir until mixture becomes thick. Remove from heat and stir in vanilla.

APPLEBEE'S MAPLE BUTTER BLONDIES

Prep time: 15 minutes | Cook time: 25 minutes | Total time: 40 minutes | Makes: 9 servings

⅓ cup butter, melted

1 cup brown sugar

1 large egg

1 tablespoon vanilla extract

½ teaspoon baking powder

⅛ teaspoon baking soda

¼ teaspoon salt

1 cup all-purpose flour

⅔ cup white chocolate chips

⅓ cup chopped pecans, plus more for topping if desired

1 recipe Maple Butter Sauce

Vanilla ice cream (optional)

Preheat oven to 350 degrees F.

In a large bowl, mix together butter, brown sugar, egg, and vanilla. Add baking powder, baking soda, salt, and flour and stir until well combined. Fold in white chocolate chips and ⅓ cup chopped pecans. Pour batter into a 9x9-inch baking dish sprayed with nonstick cooking spray. Cook 20 to 25 minutes, or until a toothpick inserted in center comes out clean. Remove blondies from oven, cut into squares, and serve with a scoop of vanilla ice cream with Maple Butter Sauce drizzled on top. Top with additional chopped pecans, if desired.

MAPLE BUTTER SAUCE

¾ cup pure maple syrup

½ cup butter

1 cup brown sugar

1 (8-ounce) package cream cheese, softened

Add maple syrup and butter to a medium saucepan over low heat and stir until melted. Add brown sugar and softened cream cheese, stirring constantly until cream cheese has melted.

DISNEYLAND MATTERHORN MACAROONS

Prep time: 15 minutes | Cook time: 15 minutes | Total time: 30 minutes | Makes: 12 macaroons

1 cup butter, softened

½ cup sugar

½ teaspoon vanilla extract

½ teaspoon coconut extract

¼ teaspoon almond extract

¼ teaspoon salt

1 (7-ounce) bag shredded, sweetened coconut flakes

2 cups all-purpose flour

2 cups white chocolate chips

Powdered sugar, for garnishing

White sprinkles, for garnishing

Preheat oven to 325 degrees F.

In a large bowl, cream together butter and sugar until light and fluffy. Add vanilla extract, coconut extract, almond extract, and salt. Mix in coconut until well combined. Fold in flour until a thick dough forms. Shape dough into small, Matterhorn-shaped heaps. Place formed dough heaps on a baking sheet, two inches apart. Bake 12 to 15 minutes, or until slightly golden brown. Let cool completely.

Pour white chocolate chips in a small bowl and microwave on high power 1 to 2 minutes or until melted, stirring every 30 seconds. Dip the top of each macaroon into the white chocolate. Garnish with powdered sugar and sprinkles while white chocolate is still hot. Let white chocolate set up before serving.

BAKED BEAR ICE CREAM COOKIE SANDWICHES

Prep time: 30 minutes | Cook time: 22 minutes | Total time: 52 minutes | Makes: 30 Ice Cream Cookie Sandwiches

24 Funfetti Cookies	36 Chocolate Chip Cookies (see recipe on page 148)
Vanilla ice cream	
Sprinkles or jimmies	Cookies and cream ice cream

Place 1 scoop of vanilla ice cream between two Funfetti Cookies. Gently press together until ice cream spreads to edge of cookies. Roll cookie sandwich edges in sprinkles. Repeat with remaining Funfetti Cookies and vanilla ice cream.

Place 1 scoop of cookies and cream ice cream between two Chocolate Chip Cookies. Gently press together until ice cream spreads to edge of cookies. Repeat with remaining Chocolate Chip Cookies and cookies and cream ice cream.

FUNFETTI COOKIES

Prep time: 10 minutes | Cook time: 10 minutes | Total time: 20 minutes | Makes: 24 cookies

½ cup butter, softened	2 cups all-purpose flour
¾ cup sugar	2 teaspoons cornstarch
1 large egg	¾ teaspoon baking soda
1½ teaspoons vanilla extract	¼ teaspoon salt
1 teaspoon almond extract	¾ cup colored sprinkles or jimmies

Preheat oven to 350 degrees F.

In a large bowl, cream together butter and sugar until light and fluffy. Beat in egg, vanilla extract, and almond extract. Fold in flour, cornstarch, baking soda, and salt and mix until well combined. Fold in sprinkles until evenly distributed. Roll dough into 1-inch balls and place on a baking sheet lined with parchment paper or a silicone baking mat. Bake 8 to 10 minutes.

Cool on a wire rack.

CHOCOLATE CHIP COOKIES

Prep time: 10 minutes | Cook time: 12 minutes | Total time: 22 minutes | Makes: 36 cookies

2¼ **cups all-purpose flour**	1 **(3.4-ounce) package instant vanilla pudding**
1 **teaspoon baking soda**	2 **eggs**
¾ **cup butter, softened**	1 **teaspoon vanilla**
¾ **cup brown sugar**	2 **cups chocolate chips**
¼ **cup granulated sugar**	

Preheat oven to 350 degrees F.

Combine flour and baking soda in a medium bowl and set aside. In a large bowl, cream together butter, brown sugar, granulated sugar, and pudding mix. Beat in eggs and vanilla. Add flour mixture and stir until combined. Fold in chocolate chips. Roll into 1-inch balls and place on a greased baking sheet. Bake 8 to 12 minutes, or until golden brown.

Cool on a wire rack.

DAIRY QUEEN BLIZZARD

Prep time: 5 minutes | Total time: 5 minutes | Makes: 2 Blizzards

- **4 cups vanilla ice cream**
- **8 Oreo Double Stuf cookies, broken into chunks**

Place frozen ice cream in a large bowl. With a hand mixer, beat the ice cream on medium speed until the ice cream is creamy but still very thick. Fold in the Oreo chunks by hand. When they are stirred in well, spoon into cups and serve with a spoon.

Note: You can add any other candy or cookie mix-ins to this Blizzard recipe.

WENDY'S FROSTY

Prep time: 5 minutes | Total time: 5 minutes | Makes: 2 servings

2   cups vanilla ice cream, slightly
    softened

⅓   cup milk

3   tablespoons Nesquik Chocolate
    Flavor Powder

1   (1.55-ounce) Hershey's Milk
    Chocolate Bar, shaved

Combine the softened ice cream, milk, and Nesquik powder in a blender. Mix until combined. Pour into 2 cups and add Hershey's bar shavings on top.

CINNABON CINNAMON ROLLS

Prep time: 5 hours | Cook time: 20 minutes | Total time: 5 hours 20 minutes | Makes: 15 cinnamon rolls

1 tablespoon active dry yeast	4 cups all-purpose flour
½ cup granulated sugar	¼ cup butter, room temperature
3 eggs, beaten	¾ cup brown sugar
1 cup lukewarm milk	2 tablespoons ground cinnamon
½ cup butter, melted	Cream Cheese Frosting
½ teaspoon salt	

Mix yeast, sugar, eggs, milk, melted butter, and salt in a large bowl. Add 4 cups all-purpose flour. Mix well with a spoon, cover bowl with plastic wrap, and allow dough to rise 4 to 6 hours or overnight in the refrigerator. Do not knead the dough.

Roll out dough into a long, thin rectangle on a lightly floured surface. Spread on ¼ cup softened butter. Mix together brown sugar and cinnamon. Spread evenly over the dough. Tightly roll into a jelly-roll shape, starting at the long end of the dough. Use a string or floss to cut dough into 1-inch pieces and place in a greased 9x13-inch baking pan. Cover and let raise an additional 30 minutes.

Preheat oven to 375 degrees F. and bake 20 to 25 minutes or until golden brown. Frost with Cream Cheese Frosting while still slightly warm.

CREAM CHEESE FROSTING

4 ounces cream cheese, softened	¼ cup butter, melted
1½ cups powdered sugar	Pinch salt
1 teaspoon vanilla extract	2 tablespoons milk

In a medium bowl, beat together cream cheese, powdered sugar, vanilla, butter, and salt until smooth.

STARBUCKS LEMON POUND CAKE

Prep time: 15 minutes | Cook time: 50 minutes | Total time: 1 hour 5 minutes | Makes: 16 servings

- 1 (15.25-ounce) box lemon cake mix
- 1 (3.4-ounce) box instant lemon pudding mix
- 1 cup sour cream
- ⅓ cup vegetable oil
- 4 eggs
- ½ cup water
- 2 tablespoons fresh lemon juice
- 1 recipe Lemon Glaze

Preheat oven to 350 degrees F. Grease and flour two 9x5-inch loaf pans.

Combine all of the cake ingredients in a large bowl and beat on medium speed with an electric mixer for 1 to 2 minutes. Pour half of the batter into each of the prepared pans. Bake 45 to 50 minutes, or until a toothpick inserted in the center of the loaf comes out clean. Let cool in the loaf pan for 30 minutes, then remove from pan and cool completely. Drizzle Lemon Glaze over the top of each loaf. Slice and serve.

LEMON GLAZE

- 1 cup powdered sugar
- 3 to 4 tablespoons lemon juice

Mix together powdered sugar and lemon juice in a small bowl, using more or less juice depending on desired consistency.

CHILI'S MOLTEN HOT LAVA CAKE

Prep time: 10 minutes | Cook time: 15 minutes | Total time: 25 minutes | Makes: 4 servings

1 cup semisweet chocolate chips

½ cup butter

1 cup powdered sugar

3 eggs

1 egg yolk

½ teaspoon vanilla extract

6 tablespoons all-purpose flour

⅛ cup caramel sauce, for drizzling

2 cups vanilla ice cream

Smucker's Chocolate Magic Shell ice cream topping, for drizzling

Preheat oven to 400 degrees F.

In a large, microwave-safe bowl, combine chocolate chips and butter. Microwave on high power for 2 minutes, stirring every 30 seconds, until smooth. Whisk in powdered sugar until combined. Add 3 eggs and 1 egg yolk and whisk until combined. Stir in vanilla and flour and mix again.

Generously spray four 1-cup oven-safe ramekins or four 1-cup fluted muffin tins with cooking spray, and evenly fill with batter. Bake on a cookie sheet in the oven 13 to 15 minutes, until the outer edges are set and the center is still soft. Remove from oven and let cool 2 to 3 minutes before inverting onto a plate drizzled with caramel sauce. Top cake with a scoop of vanilla ice cream and drizzle magic shell topping on top.

THE CHEESECAKE FACTORY WHITE CHOCOLATE TRUFFLE RASPBERRY CHEESECAKE

Prep time: 20 minutes | Cook time: 1 hour 10 minutes | Total time: 1 hour 30 minutes | Makes: 8 to 10 servings

- 12 ounces fresh raspberries
- ½ cup sugar, plus 2 tablespoons sugar
- 2 cups white chocolate chips
- ½ cup half and half
- 3 (8-ounce) packages cream cheese, softened
- 3 eggs
- 1 teaspoon vanilla extract
- 1 Oreo Crust
  White chocolate shavings

Preheat oven to 325 degrees F.

In a food processor or high-powered blender, mix together raspberries and 2 tablespoons sugar. If you prefer a seedless berry sauce, strain sauce through a mesh strainer. Set raspberry sauce aside.

In a saucepan over medium-low heat, mix together white chocolate chips and half and half until smooth and melted. Set aside.

In a large bowl, beat together cream cheese and ½ cup sugar until smooth. Beat in eggs, one at a time, then add in vanilla extract and melted white chocolate mixture. Pour half the cream cheese mixture over prepared Oreo Crust.

Swirl half the raspberry mixture in the remaining cream cheese mixture using the tip of a knife. Pour remaining cream cheese mixture over top, then swirl in the remaining raspberry mixture to create a marbled effect. Bake 55 minutes to an hour, or until edges start to brown and filling is set. Remove from the oven and let cool. Serve with white chocolate shavings.

OREO CRUST

- 18 Oreo cookies, finely crushed
- 2 teaspoons sugar
- ¼ cup butter

Preheat oven to 350 degrees F.

In a small bowl, mix together Oreo cookie crumbs, sugar, and butter until combined. Press mixture into the bottom of a 9-inch springform pan. Bake 10 minutes. Remove from the oven and let cool.

BASKIN-ROBBINS ICE CREAM CAKE

Prep time: 4 hours | Cook time: 40 minutes | Total time: 4 hours 40 minutes | Makes: 8 to 10 servings

1 (15.25-ounce) chocolate cake mix and ingredients called for on package

1 half-gallon carton chocolate chip cookie dough ice cream

Waxed paper

1 (13-ounce) bag chewy chocolate chip cookies

2¼ cups semisweet chocolate chips

¾ cup unsalted butter

Bake cake according to package directions for two 9-inch round cakes. Let cool and remove from pans.

Remove ice cream from the freezer and let it partially thaw (you don't want it to be melted, but it does need to be spreadable).

Use one of the 9-inch round cake pans to trace a circle on a large square of waxed paper. Place waxed paper on a tray or cookie sheet and spread ice cream evenly in the traced circle. Freeze until solid.

Once ice cream is frozen, remove from freezer. Place one of the 9-inch cakes on a serving plate or cake platter. Use a serrated knife to level off the top of the cake. Invert ice cream circle onto leveled-off cake and then tear off the waxed paper.

Crumble ⅔ of the package of cookies and sprinkle evenly over the ice cream. Place the second 9-inch cake on top of the cookie crumbs and press down gently. Return to freezer for 1 to 2 hours.

Before serving, heat chocolate chips and butter in a saucepan over medium heat, stirring until smooth. Pour chocolate sauce over the top of the cake, letting the sauce drip down the sides. Top cake with remaining crumbled chocolate chip cookies and serve immediately.

McDONALD'S APPLE PIE

Prep time: 15 minutes | Cook time: 30 minutes | Total time: 45 minutes | Makes: 6 hand pies

- 1 pound Granny Smith apples
- ¼ cup sugar, plus 2 tablespoons, divided
- 2 tablespoons butter
- ¾ teaspoon ground cinnamon, divided
- 5 tablespoons water, divided
- 1 tablespoon cornstarch
- 2 puff pastry sheets, thawed
- 1 egg white

Peel, core, and cut apples into ½-inch pieces. In a saucepan over medium heat, combine apples, ¼ cup sugar, butter, and ¼ teaspoon cinnamon until butter is melted, stirring often. Add 2 tablespoons water, stir to combine, then cover and cook 10 to 12 minutes, until apples are fork tender.

In a small bowl, mix together 2 tablespoons water and cornstarch to make a slurry; add slurry to saucepan. Stir and cover an additional 1 to 2 minutes, until apple mixture starts to thicken. Remove from heat and set aside.

Preheat oven to 375 degrees F.

Roll out both puff pastry sheets and cut each sheet into six 3x6-inch rectangles. Evenly distribute the apple mixture down the middle of 6 of the rectangles. Make 3 to 5 cuts down the middle of the remaining 6 sheets of puff pastry.

Top each apple-covered rectangle with a puff pastry sheet that has been cut. Press the edges together using the tines of a fork. In small bowl, mix together egg white and 1 tablespoon water. Brush egg-white mixture over the top of each hand pie. In a separate small bowl, mix together 2 tablespoons sugar and ½ teaspoon cinnamon, then sprinkle over the top of each pie.

Place on a large baking sheet and bake 15 to 18 minutes, until pastry starts to brown.

NESTLÉ TOLLHOUSE COOKIE PIE

Prep time: 10 minutes | Cook time: 50 minutes | Total time: 1 hour | Makes: 8 servings

- 1 unbaked 9-inch pie crust, homemade or store-bought.
- 2 large eggs
- ½ cup all-purpose flour
- ½ cup granulated sugar
- ½ cup packed brown sugar
- ¾ cup butter, softened
- 1 cup semisweet chocolate chips
- 1 cup chopped pecans (optional)

Preheat oven to 325 degrees F. Line a 9-inch pie plate with prepared crust; set aside.

Beat eggs in large mixer bowl on high speed until foamy. Beat in flour, granulated sugar, and brown sugar. Beat in butter. Stir in morsels and nuts. Spoon into pie shell.

Bake 50 to 55 minutes or until knife inserted halfway between edge and center comes out clean. Cool on wire rack or serve slightly warmed. Serve with ice cream or whipped cream. You can also drizzle chocolate syrup on top!

TACO TIME PUMPKIN EMPANADAS

Prep time: 10 Minutes | Cook time: 5 Minutes | Total time: 15 minutes | Makes: 8 empanadas

1 (8-ounce) package cream cheese, room temperature

1 cup sugar, divided

1 cup canned pumpkin

1 teaspoon vanilla

2 teaspoons pumpkin pie spice

8 flour tortillas

Vegetable or canola oil, for frying

2 tablespoons ground cinnamon

Nondairy whipped topping or freshly whipped cream, for dipping

In a large bowl with an electric mixer, cream together cream cheese and ½ cup sugar until smooth. Blend in canned pumpkin, vanilla, and pumpkin pie spice.

Put about ⅓ cup of pumpkin filling in the center of each tortilla; spread filling almost to the edges. Roll up carefully and secure with a toothpick.

Heat 1 to 2 inches of oil in a large pot to 350 degrees F. Drop empanadas in hot oil and fry until golden brown, about 2 minutes. Place on paper towels to drain excess oil. Remove toothpicks.

In a shallow bowl, combine ½ cup sugar and 2 tablespoons cinnamon. Roll hot empanadas in mixture and serve warm. Serve with whipped topping or fresh whipped cream, for dipping.

OLIVE GARDEN CREAM CAKE

Prep time: 25 minutes | Cook time: 45 minutes | Total time: 1 hour 10 minutes | Makes: 8 servings

1 **(18-ounce) box white cake mix**

4 **egg whites**

1 **cup water**

⅓ **cup oil**

1 **tablespoon fresh lemon juice**

Zest of 1 lemon

1 **recipe Lemon Cream Filling**

1 **recipe Crumb Topping**

Preheat oven to 350 degrees F. Grease and flour a 9-inch springform pan.

Combine cake mix, water, oil, egg whites, lemon juice, and lemon zest. Pour into prepared pan. Bake 40 to 45 minutes.

Allow cake to cool for 20 minutes, then remove edges of pan and allow to cool fully.

Slice cake in half horizontally. Spread half of the Lemon Cream Filling on top of bottom cake half. Put cake back together and spread remaining Lemon Cream Filling on top of cake.

Sprinkle top with Crumb Topping and refrigerate until ready to serve.

LEMON CREAM FILLING

1 **(8-ounce) package cream cheese, softened**

2½ **cups powdered sugar**

1 **tablespoon fresh lemon juice**

1 **cup heavy cream**

Combine cream cheese, powdered sugar, and lemon juice in a large bowl and beat with an electric mixer until smooth.

Whip cream until stiff peaks form, and then fold into cream cheese mixture.

CRUMB TOPPING

1 **cup powdered sugar**

1 **cup all-purpose flour**

3 **tablespoons butter, softened**

1 **teaspoon vanilla**

Zest of 1 lemon

Combine all ingredients in bowl of food processor and pulse until mixture resembles coarse crumbs.

SPRINKLES RED VELVET CUPCAKES

Prep time: 25 minutes | Cook time: 20 minutes | Total time: 45 minutes | Makes: 15 cupcakes

- 1⅓ cups all-purpose flour
- 3 tablespoons cocoa powder
- ½ teaspoon baking soda
- ¾ cup butter, room temperature
- 1 cup sugar
- 2 large eggs
- 1 tablespoon red food coloring
- 2 teaspoons vanilla extract
- ½ cup whole milk
- 1 teaspoon distilled white vinegar
- 1 recipe Cream Cheese Frosting
- Red and blue food coloring (optional)

Preheat oven to 350 degrees F.

In a mixing bowl, whisk together flour, cocoa powder, and baking soda. In a separate large mixing bowl, beat together the butter and sugar with an electric mixer until fluffy, about 3 to 4 minutes. Add in eggs and mix. Add red food coloring and vanilla extract and mix until combined.

In a small mixing bowl, combine milk and 1 teaspoon vinegar. Add milk mixture and flour mixture to batter and stir well to combine.

Divide batter evenly among 15 paper-lined muffin cups, filling each cup about ⅔ full. Bake for 18 to 21 minutes, until toothpick inserted in center of cupcake comes out clean. Remove from oven and allow to cool.

Once cooled completely, spread tops generously with Cream Cheese Frosting, reserving a small amount of frosting to color and use to make the famous Sprinkles design.

Divide reserved frosting between 2 small bowls. Color one bowl red and the other blue. Frost a small red circle in the middle of each cupcake. Frost a smaller blue circle in the middle of each red circle.

CREAM CHEESE FROSTING

- ½ cup butter, room temperature
- 6 ounces cream cheese, softened
- 1 teaspoon vanilla extract
- 3½ cups powdered sugar

Using an electric mixer, beat together butter and cream cheese until pale and fluffy. Mix in vanilla extract and powdered sugar and beat until smooth, about 3 minutes.

THE CHEESECAKE FACTORY PUMPKIN CHEESECAKE

Prep time: 20 | Cook time: 1 hour 15 minutes | Total time: 1 hour 35 minutes | Makes: 8 servings

1½ cups graham cracker crumbs

5 tablespoons butter, melted

1 cup sugar, plus 1 tablespoon sugar

3 (8-ounce) packages cream cheese

1 teaspoon vanilla

1 cup canned pumpkin

3 eggs

½ teaspoon ground cinnamon

¼ teaspoon ground nutmeg

¼ teaspoon ground allspice

Preheat oven to 350 degrees F.

Combine the graham cracker crumbs with the melted butter and 1 tablespoon sugar in a medium bowl.

Press the crumbs onto the bottom and about ⅔ up the sides of a 9-inch springform pan. Bake the crust 5 minutes, then set aside while you make the filling.

In a large mixing bowl, combine the cream cheese, 1 cup of sugar, and vanilla. Beat with an electric mixer until smooth.

Add the pumpkin, eggs, cinnamon, nutmeg, and allspice and continue beating until smooth and creamy.

Pour the filling carefully into the prepared pan.

Bake 60 to 70 minutes. The top will be a little bit browner than the rest. Remove it from the oven and allow the cheesecake to cool.

When the cheesecake has come to room temperature, chill in the refrigerator at least 4 hours. Remove the pan sides and cut the cake into 8 equal pieces.

Serve with your favorite toppings, such as whipped cream and caramel sauce!

DISNEY GRAHAMS

Prep time: 1 hour | Total time: 1 hour | Makes: 12 servings

3   cups milk chocolate chips, divided

2   teaspoons shortening, divided

6   graham cracker sheets, broken in half

1   cup creamy peanut butter

½   cup powdered sugar

½   teaspoon vanilla

1½   teaspoons milk

Line a cookie sheet with waxed paper or parchment paper.

Melt 1½ cups of the chocolate chips and 1 teaspoon of the shortening in a microwave-safe bowl on high power, stirring every 30 seconds, until fully melted and smooth.

Dip each graham cracker half into the chocolate, tapping or gently scraping off the excess chocolate, but ensuring that the whole cracker is covered.

Set each chocolate-covered graham cracker on the cookie sheet and place in the refrigerator or freezer to set up quickly.

While the chocolate-covered graham crackers are setting up, make the peanut butter filling by mixing the peanut butter, powdered sugar, vanilla, and milk. Mix until smooth. Roll into 12 equal dough balls and chill in the freezer for about 15 minutes.

Pull out the chilled chocolate-covered graham crackers and peanut butter balls. Gently flatten the peanut butter balls to the size of the graham cracker and place it on the chocolate graham. Gently spread it to the edges so it's evenly distributed.

Melt the other 1½ cups chocolate chips with 1 teaspoon of shortening, stirring until smooth. Gently spoon chocolate over the peanut butter layer and spread around with a spoon, covering the top and sides. Put back in the fridge or freezer to set up, about 15 to 20 minutes.

Store in the refrigerator in an airtight container for up to a week; set at room temp for about 20 minutes before eating.

Drinks

DISNEYLAND DOLE WHIP FLOAT

Prep time: 2 hours 5 minutes | Makes: 4 servings

- 1 (16-ounce) bag frozen pineapple chunks
- 4 cups vanilla ice cream
- 1 teaspoon lime juice
- 1 teaspoon lemon juice
- 1½ cups pineapple juice

Puree frozen pineapple in a blender. Add ice cream, lime juice, lemon juice, and half the pineapple juice. Blend together until smooth. Place mixture in the freezer for 2 hours to set up. Scoop or pipe into glasses and pour remaining pineapple juice over each serving.

RED ROBIN FRECKLED LEMONADE

Prep time: 10 minutes | Cook time: 5 minutes | Total time: 15 minutes | Makes: 8 servings

2	**quarts water**
½	**cup sugar**
¾	**cup lemon juice**
2	**cups frozen strawberries in syrup**

In a large pot, combine water and sugar. Stir over medium heat until sugar dissolves. Remove from heat and mix in lemon juice. Add frozen strawberries to a blender and puree. Mix into lemonade and chill in refrigerator until ready to serve. Add additional frozen strawberries to lemonade as a garnish, if desired.

THE DRINK SHOP DIET COKE

Prep time: 5 minutes | Total time: 5 minutes | Makes: 4 servings

- **4 cups crushed ice**
- **4 (12-ounce) cans Diet Coke**
- **8 tablespoons coconut syrup**
- **2 tablespoons heavy cream**
- **2 limes, halved**

Place one cup of ice in each of 4 separate glasses. Fill each glass with 12 ounces Diet Coke. To each glass, stir in 2 tablespoons coconut syrup and ½ tablespoon heavy cream. Squeeze half a lime into each glass, then top each drink with additional lime wedges and serve.

KNEADERS SNOWBERRY STEAMER

Prep time: 5 minutes | Cook time: 5 minutes | Total time: 10 minutes | Makes: 2 servings

½ **cup white chocolate chips**

½ **cup fresh or frozen raspberries**

2 **cups milk**

Hazelnut syrup to taste

In a medium saucepan on medium-low heat, stir white chocolate chips and raspberries until they have melted together. Add in the milk and stir until you can start to see steam rise from the milk. Remove from the heat and stir in the hazelnut syrup. Serve immediately.

SONIC DRIVE-IN SLUSH

Prep time: 5 minutes | Total time: 5 minutes | Makes: 4 servings

4   **cups ice**

2   **cups lemon-lime soda**

2   **packets blue-raspberry lemonade Kool-Aid**

¼   **cup sugar**

In a high-powered blender, blend ice until it is finely crushed. Add lemon-lime soda, Kool-Aid, and sugar and pulse until completely combined. Pour into four cups and serve.

CHICK-FIL-A FROSTED LEMONADE

Prep time: 10 minutes | Total time: 10 minutes | Makes: 2 servings

1 cup fresh-squeezed lemon juice	**1 quart vanilla ice cream**
½ cup sugar	**1 lemon**
2½ cups ice-cold water	

Mix the lemon juice and sugar together in a pitcher and stir until the sugar is dissolved. Add in the ice-cold water and stir until it is well mixed. Pour 1 cup of the lemonade mixture and 2 cups of vanilla ice cream into a blender. Blend together and pour into 2 cups and garnish with a lemon slice. You can repeat the directions by adding more ice cream to the lemonade mixture.

UNIVERSAL STUDIOS BUTTERBEER

Prep time: 2 hours 10 minutes | Total time: 2 hours 10 minutes | Makes: 4

1 liter cream soda

3 teaspoons imitation butter extract

2 cups vanilla ice cream, softened

Freeze ½ of the soda in ice cube trays for about 2 hours.

When soda is frozen, add soda ice cubes, 2 teaspoons butter extract, and the remaining half of the cream soda to a blender jar and blend well. Pour cream soda mixture into your favorite mugs. In the blender, beat the softened ice cream and remaining teaspoon of butter extract until smooth. Pour ice cream mixture on top of Butterbeer for a frothy finish.

SONIC DRIVE-IN CHERRY LIMEADE

Prep time: 5 minutes | Total time: 5 minutes | Makes: 6 servings

1 (12-ounce) can frozen limeade concentrate

1 (2-liter) bottle lemon-lime soda

Juice from 1 (10-ounce) jar maraschino cherries

2 cups crushed ice

Fresh limes, sliced

6 to 12 maraschino cherries

Mix together the frozen limeade concentrate, lemon-lime soda, and cherry juice. Pour into glasses, add crushed ice to each glass, and top off with a fresh lime slice and 1 to 2 maraschino cherries.

ORANGE JULIUS

Prep time: 5 minutes | Total time: 5 minutes | Makes: 4 servings

- **6** **ounces frozen orange juice concentrate**
- **1½** **cups milk**
- **½** **cup water**
- **¼** **cup sugar**
- **1** **teaspoon vanilla**
- **2** **tablespoons powdered sugar**

Combine all ingredients in a high-powered blender and blend until smooth.

TACO BELL PIÑA COLADA FRUTISTA

Total time: 10 minutes | Makes: 2 servings

- **1 cup crushed ice**
- **1 cup piña colada mix**
- **½ cup lemon-lime soda**
- **2 lime slices**

Place ice, piña colada mix, and soda into the blender and blend until smooth. Pour into 2 glasses and top each with a lime slice. Serve immediately.

GHIRARDELLI HOT CHOCOLATE

Prep time: 5 minutes | Cook time: 5 minutes | Total time: 10 minutes | Makes: 4 servings

4 cups milk

1 cup Ghirardelli semisweet chocolate chips

Whipped topping

Combine milk and chocolate in saucepan over medium heat. Stir constantly with metal whisk until all chocolate is melted.

Serve with whipped topping.

JAMBA JUICE MANGO-A-GO-GO

Prep time: 5 minutes | Total time: 5 minutes | Makes: 2 servings

1 cup mango juice

1 cup pineapple sherbet

1½ cups frozen mangoes

½ cup ice

Blend all ingredients together in blender and serve.

CHICK-FIL-A LEMONADE

Prep time: 15 minutes | Total time: 15 minutes | Makes: 5 servings

2 **cups freshly squeezed lemon juice (about 8 to 10 lemons)**

1½ **cups sugar**

6 **cups water**

Combine all ingredients in pitcher and stir until combined. Best if served cold!

A&W ROOT BEER

Prep time: 5 minutes | Cook time: 10 minutes | Total time: 15 minutes | Makes: 4 servings

- ¾ **cup sugar**
- ¼ **cup hot water**
- ½ **teaspoon root beer concentrate**
- 4 **cups cold seltzer water**

Dissolve sugar in hot water. Add root beer flavoring. Slowly add to seltzer water and serve over ice.

DISNEYLAND MINT JULEP

Prep time: 40 minutes | Cook time: 10 minutes | Total time: 50 minutes | Makes: 8 servings

- 1 **cup sugar**
- 3 **cups club soda**
- 3 **teaspoons limeade concentrate**
- 6 **ounces frozen lemonade concentrate, thawed**
- 4 **tablespoons crème de menthe syrup (not liqueur) OR 3 drops mint extract mixed with 2 tablespoons water**
- **Mint leaves**
- **Pineapple slices**
- **Maraschino cherries**
- **Toothpicks**

In a large saucepan, mix sugar and soda over medium heat until sugar is dissolved. Add lime juice and lemonade and bring mixture to a boil.

Once boiling, remove from heat and add crème de menthe syrup or a mixture of 3 drops mint extract with 2 tablespoons water.

Chill in fridge 30 minutes to an hour.

For a 2-cup serving, mix ½ cup mixture with 1½ cups of water.

Serve with cherries and pineapple slices on a toothpick and mint leaves for a garnish.

Index

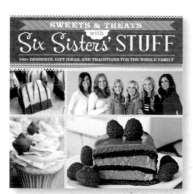
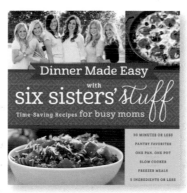